Happy fungus hunting
from Nick

Mushrooms
in the **Wild**

Mushrooms
in the Wild

edited by Ian Tribe

ORBIS PUBLISHING·LONDON

Frontispiece: Pholiota squarrosa (S. C. Porter/Bruce Coleman)
Endpapers: Clitocybe clavipes (Eric Hosking)

© Istituto Geografico de Agostini S.p.A., Novara 1976
English Language Edition © Orbis Publishing Limited, London 1977
All rights reserved
Printed in Italy by IGDA, Novara
ISBN: 0 85613 016 8

Contents

Introduction

Our lives today are a far cry from a century ago. One predictable result of the vast changes in our surroundings and living conditions is that many who have tasted the dubious delights of modernity are returning to old values and rural customs such as herbal remedies, country crafts and 'genuine' foods.

The upsurge of interest in fungi is a reflection of this revolt against a world of convenience foods and labour-saving gadgetry. This presents problems for the beginner estranged from his rural heritage. Inaccurate identification can be lethal if the wrong fungus is picked and eaten, and no gatherer should touch a fungus if he is in the slightest doubt of its identity. However, that should not discourage the enthusiast. Although it may take a while to become familiar with even the commoner types of fungus and to become confident of one's identification, the rewards for perseverance are absorbing walks in town and country and an enriched diet.

This book sets out to show the reader a representative range of common and interesting fungi, with a guide to their edibility, and, perhaps more important, it also relates these fungi to their natural habitat. Many books help the layman to identify fungi, but very few go on to discuss where they grow and why. This ecological approach has an importance wider than the study of fungi; for, as this book shows, it is impossible to look at one kind of plant or animal in its environment without considering the environment generally—a vital consideration in a world increasingly disfigured by industrialization.

Ian Tribe

This beautiful species, Flammulina velutipes, is found on the stumps, trunks and branches of trees

The Elusive Mushroom

Fungi are usually regarded as plants, yet they appear suddenly and mysteriously, often overnight, out of the soil or from tree trunks. Their sudden appearance has, in the past, provoked talk of 'spontaneous generation'. This old theory, common before the work of Pasteur, stated that micro-organisms were capable of appearing from nowhere and out of nothing. The appearance of fungi, however, has nothing to do with magic. What we see as the fungus is only a fruiting body— one stage of a complex life history that takes place mostly underground. The damp of autumn, or the warmth of spring are usually adequate to trigger fungi into producing their fruiting bodies, giving a sudden 'flush' of fungi at these times of the year.

They appear in virtually every colour, from snow-white to flame-red, and lemon-yellow to vivid orange; there is certainly no shortage of brown or ochreous, grey, black or violet shades. Blue and green mushrooms are rare and come in rather pale hues, usually greyish-blue where the former are concerned, and tending to olive-green in the latter. Indeed mushrooms present such a wide range of colour and form that many artists have chosen them as subjects for still-life paintings or book illustrations.

Plant or animal?

It is perhaps surprising that fungi should be considered as plants, since they lack chlorophyll—the green pigment found in plants which absorbs energy from sunlight. Furthermore they share a number of features in common with animals. For example, their cell walls are partly composed of fungal chitin, which is similar to the horny chitin found in many animals. Like animals, mushrooms and toadstools are incapable of manufacturing their own food; whereas plants gain nourishment out of carbon dioxide from the air, and water from the soil, using sunlight as a source of energy. Some types of fungus are even capable of swarming over soil, like simple animals.

At the same time, fungi have many plant-like features, such as the possession of cell walls. The situation is so confused that a number of biologists have proposed that fungi ought to be grouped quite separately as a third Kingdom distinct from plants and animals. There are good arguments for such a proposal, but it causes confusion with a public that considers fungi as plants.

The parts of the mushroom

If one dissects a mushroom it can be seen that its stalk, technically termed a stipe, and its cap, or pileus, usually have a distinct texture. The flesh may be firm or rather soft and is sometimes watery. It does not display distinct specific structures, and under a microscope, a thin sliver of mushroom flesh appears to consist of a tightly packed conglomeration of extremely fine microscopic filaments, which are transparent.

Right: Amanita phalloides, showing the 'egg' and the expanded fruiting body of this lethal species
Above right: Russula nigricans, an example of a gilled fungus

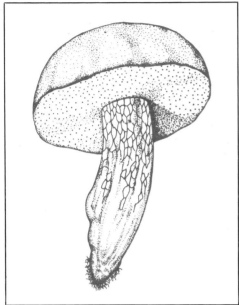

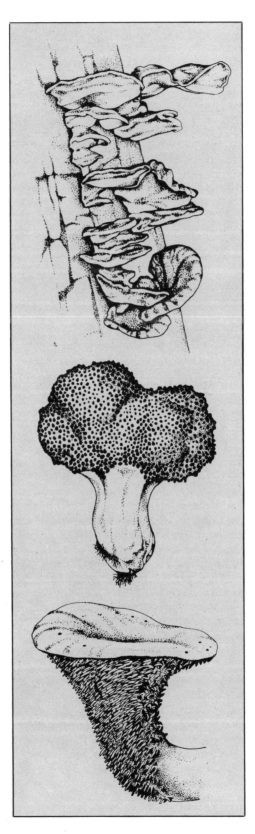

Some of the strange shapes found among the Basidiomycetes
Far left: Boletus luridus
Left: Polyporus sulfureus
Centre: Polyporus pes-caprae
Bottom: Hydnum repandum

Each one of these filaments is a hypha and hyphae form not only the body, or thallus, of the fungus, but also the mycelium, which is the less evident part forming a cobweb-like veil which grows over or through soil or bark. The mycelium is the part of the fungus which can be regarded as the plant, whereas what we usually call 'a mushroom' is a fruit-bearing body that carries the spores. These spores, given the right conditions, germinate and give rise to the development of a new mycelium. It is the mycelium which obtains food for the plant by taking in dissolved substances or by secreting enzymes. These break down complex materials such as wood and cellulose into soluble food which can be absorbed. Each hypha of which the mycelium is composed is formed by very long cells joined together to make the filament. Inside every cell are rounded bodies called nuclei—which control its vital functions. There are also septa or cross-walls which separate one cell from the next, and other microscopic structures such as drops and granules.

The mycelium originating from the germinated spore is called the primary mycelium and, as may be imagined, the ground in a wood may be covered with countless primary mycelia all belonging to different species of fungi. Since a single fungus may be capable of producing several million spores, a fertile habitat will contain a

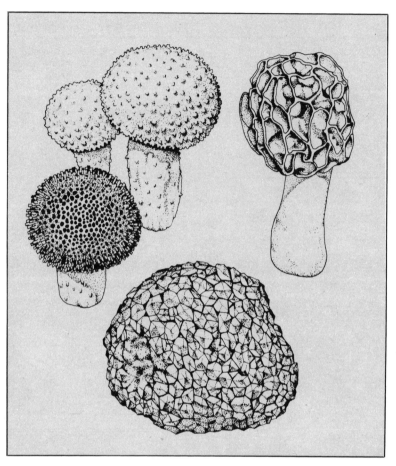

pores, each one of which is actually the mouth of a very thin tubule. Tubules form the entire lower part of the cap; they are so numerous that they resemble a sort of sponge which is firm to begin with, and then becomes less so as the pores develop. This type is found among a large group of *Boletus* species.

The third type has a mass of spines in place of gills or pores and is found in *Hydnum* species. There are other variations, but gills, pores or spines, volva and ring are the main features which enable most of the larger fungus species to be distinguished. There are also intermediate forms between the Agarics (with gills) and the Boleti (with pores), with pores which are not round but angular or elongated, or gills more or less reduced to the size of pleats or folds, as in the case of the handsome Chantarelle. Some fungi have no stipe at all, usually growing on tree trunks, while others, such as the Morels, have a honeycomb-like cap or one which is club or coral-shaped.

Spores
Spores are a further distinctive feature of mushrooms which can be used to distinguish species. They are microscopic, single-celled, bodies either rounded, oval, spindle-like or angular in shape. Spores may be transparent

Above: Three similar-looking types which are very different. The two Lycoperdon species (top left) are Basidiomycetes and the Morchella (top right) and Tuber species are Ascomycetes
Right: Fungal hyphae are made up of separate cells joined end to end. The round objects are nuclei

multitude of different mycelia. These frequently and inevitably come into contact and occasionally a special process of fusion will occur. This happens when two mycelia of the same species come into contact with each other, giving rise to sexual fusion. This initial process is eventually followed by the formation of a fungus body from the secondary or advanced mycelium.

Three types of cap fungi
There are three principal types of structure found in larger fungi which have caps. The first has an elegant array of gills beneath the cap, a stalk with a skirt-like ring at the top, and at the base a membranous cup or 'volva' enveloping it. This type is best represented by the Amanitas; other gilled fungi, known collectively as Agarics, may lack either a volva or a ring, or both.

The second type has a stipe with no volva or ring; on the lower surface of the cap there are no gills, but countless perforations called

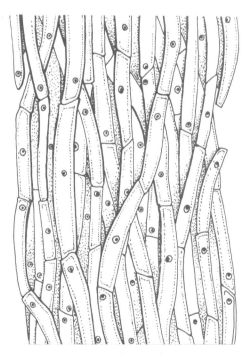

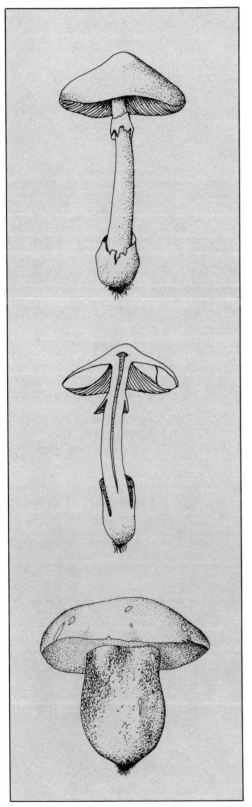

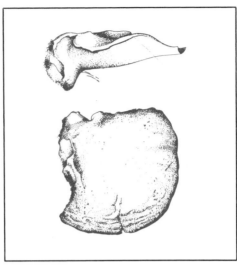

Left: The Beefsteak Fungus, a Polypore, grows on tree trunks
Far left: The typical Amanita, (top and centre) has a ring and volva. The squat Bolete (bottom), typically, has no ring or volva and a spongy mass of tubes under the cap

or coloured, and are produced in tens of millions in every sort of fungus, on the gills, inside the tubes, or on the outer surface of the spines, alveolae and fruiting bodies. The spores of larger fungi are produced by specialized cells. In the Morels, for example, the spores are contained in miscroscopic, elongated cells called asci, and are termed ascospores. Fungi having these asci (singular ascus) are Ascomycetes, to which Truffles also belong.

Those fungi with gills, pores and spines, on the other hand, belong to the Basidiomycetes because the spores, termed basidiospores, are carried at the tips of club-shaped cells called basidia. Both asci and basidia form a close fertile layer known as the hymenium.

It is evident that the two major terms used above have a common ending, 'mycetes', from the Greek *mykes* meaning fungus. This is why the science of studying these organisms is called mycology, and those engaged in such study are known as mycologists. Mycology is a very important discipline because of the economic significance of fungi. They have both good and bad effects, being used to make antibiotics, for example, but also being responsible for many diseases in plants and animals. Mycologists are kept very busy with these problems and with the task of classifying new species. For all the apparent simplicity of these organisms, fungi conceal biological problems which are still far from being solved.

The Classification of Fungi

In common with all other living organisms, it is possible to classify fungi though this is, of course, not as easy as it sounds. The fungi are generally very varied, so that it is often very difficult to know how they are related—that is, whether they belong to the same family or to totally different groups, and which appeared in evolution first. Classification should, after all, reflect natural relationships, or evolution, as closely as possible. There are also many fungi, grouped solely for convenience as the Fungi Imperfecti or Deuteromycetes, where the life-cycle is not properly known or is literally incomplete.

The system of Latin names devised by Linnaeus is designed to identify any organism by a system which may be applied the world over. This enables the fungi, for instance, to be named uniformly, whether the species occurs in North America or France. These names are internationally recognised, so that living things can be identified in the same way all over the world. To use English names only would cause confusion, and would not be internationally understood. Most fungi do not, in fact, have English names, so there is no alternative but to use the scientific ones. The English names used in this book are those in general use. Another justification for such classification is that it is important to know how fungi are related; in other words, how they have evolved. In recent years our knowledge of fungi has increased significantly, and as a result there have been many changes of classification. This temporarily leads to some chaos, but provided that the original Latin names (synonyms) are also quoted, it is not difficult to follow. There are various systems of fungal classification at present in use, and there is no point in mentioning but one. The system used in this book is that adopted by Vignoli (1964).

Ascomycetes and Basidiomycetes

This book is not concerned with the multitude of miscroscopic fungi. The larger fungi belong to two principal classes, the Ascomycetes and Basidiomycetes, which are distinguished by the type of spore and the manner in which it is produced. Of the two classes, the Basidiomycetes are the more easily visible and are thought to be more highly evolved.

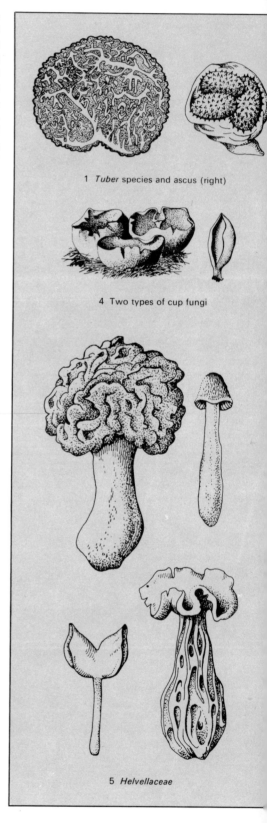

1 *Tuber* species and ascus (right)

4 Two types of cup fungi

5 *Helvellaceae*

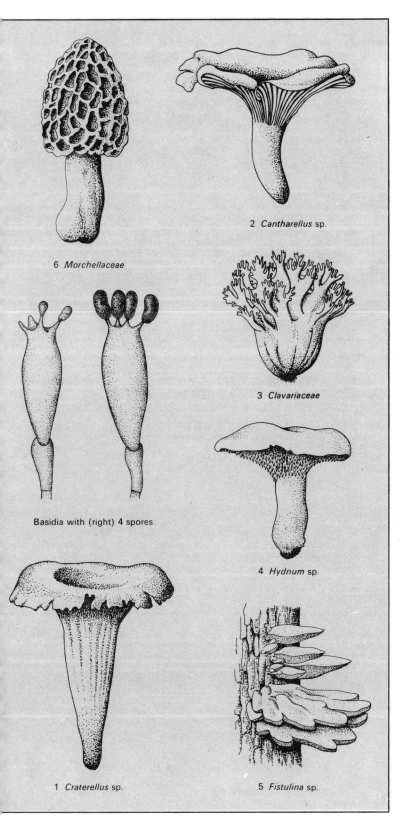

6 *Morchellaceae*

2 *Cantharellus* sp.

3 *Clavariaceae*

Basidia with (right) 4 spores

4 *Hydnum* sp.

1 *Craterellus* sp.

5 *Fistulina* sp.

ASCOMYCETES
Sexual spores are produced inside an ascus (hyphae septate). They include the yeasts, truffles, certain mildews and Morels.

1 *Family Tuberaceae*: subterranean with fruiting bodies of varied shape and colour; gleba often marbled; internal chambers connect with outside. Typical genus—*Tuber*.

2 *Family Terfeziaceae*: very similar to true truffles, but gleba with no direct connection with the exterior. Typical genus—*Terfezia*.

3 *Family Elaphomycetaceae*: subterranean fungi, rounded; gleba protected by skin (peridium), covered by a yellowish brown layer. Typical genus—*Elaphomyces*.

4 *Family Pezizaceae*: hymenium lines inner surface of cup. Typical genus—*Peziza*.

5 *Family Helvellaceae*: stipe cylindrical or etched; cap lobed but not honeycombed; spores 8, elliptical. Typical genera—*Helvella, Gyromitra, Verpa*.

6 *Family Morchellaceae*: characterized by hollow stipe and honeycombed, mitre-shaped cap; spores 8. Typical genus—*Morchella*.

BASIDIOMYCETES
Sexual spores are produced on a basidium (hyphae septate). They include Agarics, club fungi, bracket fungi and Boletes.

1 *Family Thelephoraceae*: fruiting bodies trumpet or coral-shaped, with an external hymenium. Typical genus—*Craterellus*.

2 *Family Cantharellaceae*: fruiting body with stalk and cap, slightly eccentric and lobed; decurrent gill-like structures contain the hymenium. Typical genus—*Cantharellus*.

3 *Family Clavariceae*: fruiting bodies coral- or club-shaped. Typical genera—*Clavaria, Sparassis*.

4 *Family Hydnaceae*: fruiting body with stalk and cap; hymenium covers warts, teeth or spines. Typical genus—*Hydnum*.

5 *Family Fistulinaceae*: bracket or shelf-shaped, on trees (hymenium on lower surface). Lining shallow tubes not easily distinguished from flesh. Typical genus—*Fistulina*.

13

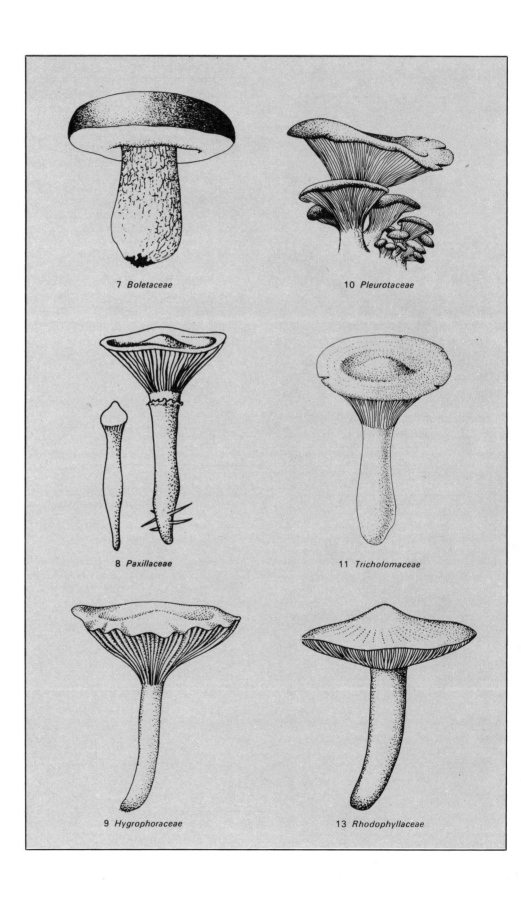

7 *Boletaceae*

10 *Pleurotaceae*

8 *Paxillaceae*

11 *Tricholomaceae*

9 *Hygrophoraceae*

13 *Rhodophyllaceae*

6 *Family Polyporaceae:* bracket-shaped, with or without stipe, on trees. Hymenium lining tubes cannot easily be removed from flesh. Typical genera—*Fomes, Polyporus, Daedalea, Ganoderma, Trametes.*

7 *Family Boletaceae:* closely allied with gilled fungi, not polypores. Usually soil-dwelling with cap and stipe and no ring. Tubes, containing hymenium, are easily removed from flesh. The family *Strobilomycetaceae* is very closely allied. Typical genus *Boletus.*

8 *Family Paxillaceae:* gills frequently united by conspicuous veins. Gills separate easily from flesh, as in *Boletaceae.* Typical species—*Paxillus.*

9 *Family Hygrophoraceae:* fleshy fruiting body with waxy, triangular gills. Typical genus—*Hygrophorus.*

10 *Family Pleurotaceae:* corticolous species with an eccentric cap, frequently without a stipe. Typical genus—*Pleurotus.*

11 *Family Tricholomaceae:* cap continuous with stipe. Gills unequal in length, spores white. Typical genus—*Tricholoma.*

12 *Family Marasmiaceae:* small fungi with distant, membranous gills and slender stipe. Typical genus—*Marasmius.*

13 *Family Rhodophyllaceae:* large family of varied shape and size. Spores rose or salmon-coloured, polygonal, or angular; terrestrial. Typical genus—*Rhodophyllus, Entoloma* (the latter being now usually regarded as synonymous with the former).

14 *Family Cortinariaceae:* typified by the presence of a veil (cortina) between cap and stipe. This is a derivative of the partial veil enclosing the gills in the juvenile stage; spores rusty-brown. Typical genus—*Cortinarius.*

15 *Family Coprinaceae:* auto-digestion of cap releases inky mass of black or dark brown spores. Cap frequently scaly. Typical genus—*Coprinus.*

16 *Family Agaricaceae:* a large family with white spores. A ring is usually present and a volva occasionally. The cap is easily separated from the stipe. The family includes the true mushrooms. Typical genera—*Amanita, Agaricus, Lepiota.*

14 *Cortinariaceae*

15 *Coprinaceae*

16 *Agaricaceae*

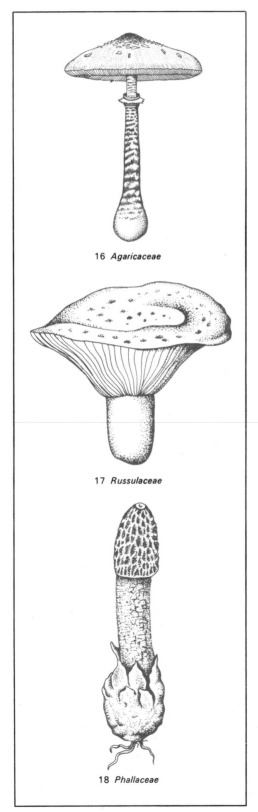

16 *Agaricaceae*

17 *Russulaceae*

18 *Phallaceae*

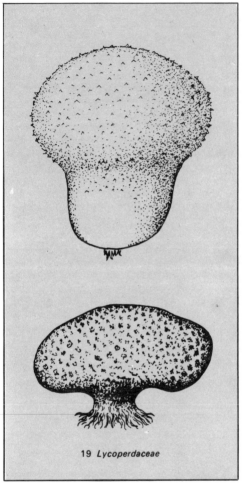

19 *Lycoperdaceae*

17 *Family Russulaceae:* large and varied family with white or yellow spores. The cap is usually depressed at maturity. Two genera—*Russula*, with no latex and brittle stipe, and *Lactarius*, with latex. Taste important in identification.

18 *Family Phallaceae:* fruiting body initially egg-shaped, later expanding to expose the gleba in a variety of ways. Their smell is strong and distinctive, apparently to attract insects for spore dispersal. Typical genera—*Phallus, Mutinus*.

19 *Family Lycoperdaceae:* globose fungi with internal gleba, with or withour integrated stipe. Outer layer is warty or spiny. Typical genus—*Lycoperdon*.

20 *Family Sclerodermaceae:* thick-skinned, opening by cracking. These fungi are sessile with gleba typically purplish. Typical genera—*Scleroderma*, Earthballs.

The Place of the Mushroom

If the numerous microscopic or inconspicuous species such as the moulds or mildews are included in the general classification 'fungi', then it can be said that these organisms are more or less in evidence everywhere, growing in all types of organic material, particularly those in the process of decomposition or fermentation. The various types of yeast used in making wine, vinegar, beer and bread are fungi. The moulds and mildews found on paper, leather, preserves, and fruit in general are also fungi. Even more surprising, fungi are the cause of the whitish layers which cover the mucous membranes in babies' mouths, giving rise to so-called 'thrush', and of athletes' foot and ringworm which affect the skin.

Recycling and disease

Similarly, fungi are the cause of the numerous and often extremely harmful diseases which afflict many cultivated plants: cereal rusts, maize smuts, ergot of rye, pear and apple scabs, and club-root in cabbages. There is also a vast range of fungi which blemish, deform and wilt the leaves of vegetables, fruit and ornamental trees.

Much of the work of recycling materials in nature is, in fact, performed by microscopic soil and water fungi. The higher fungi are often responsible for a vital part of this recycling and tend to be specialized for a particular function; killing a host plant, or initiating the breakdown of a tree trunk, for example. This partly explains why Field Mushrooms are never found in woods, and similarly, why the Wood Mushroom is never found in pasture: they are adapted to different circumstances and requirements.

The same effect can be seen in the distribution of higher plants: in open places poppies and the Ox-Eye Daisy are to be found, whereas in woods one finds Wood Anemone, Bluebells and Sweet Violets, although these do sometimes stray from their typical habitats. For these plants the principal factors governing their lives are shade, humidity, warmth and soil conditions such as humus and acid content. Plant species are often associated in communities which may be typical of certain conditions: heathland, chalk grassland and beech woods for example.

In the case of fungi, however, their circumstances are frequently complicated by the nature of the plant species growing in a habitat and by the amount and type of decaying material. Most woodland fungi are associated with the trees and are thus dependent on them. Some of these fungi are very specific in their requirements and grow exclusively in, for example, beech woods, pine woods or oak woods.

Saprophytic and mycorrhizal fungi

Their nutritional requirements make it possible to divide the larger fungi into two major groups. The first includes the saprophytic species—fungi which live on decayed organic matter. These grow in large numbers on organic compost, in meadows where

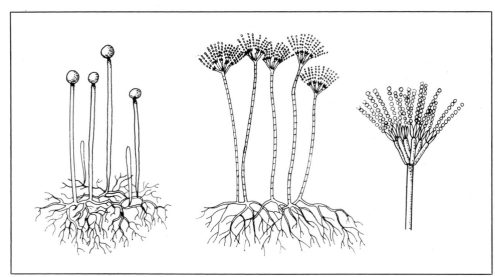

Left: These are the fruiting bodies of two conidiophore moulds

17

Right: These are the cells of the yeast mould Saccharomyces cerevusuae, seen under magnification
Below: Diseases of pears (top) and maize (bottom) are two of the many caused by microscopic fungi

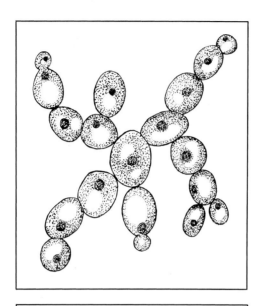

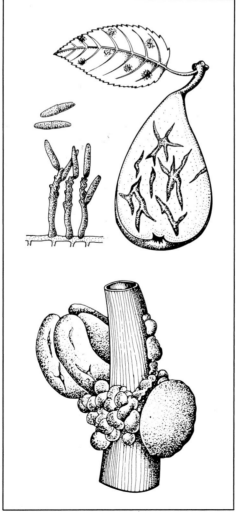

there may be manure, or on stumps or tree-trunks, developing in places where a spore has landed, and germinated, and the mycelium has subsequently developed.

The second and more complex group is composed of fungi which mycologists call 'mycorrhizal' because they develop their mycelium until it touches the roots of trees and completely envelops them, forming a mycorrhiza. The mycorrhiza may even penetrate the tree's root cells, forming a very close link with the tree. This arrangement does not harm the tree, as both fungus and tree benefit from the other's activities. The tree, which is capable of manufacturing its own food, supplies sugars and other food substances to the fungus, in exchange for water and mineral salts absorbed by the fungus. These fungi have a greater ability to extract minerals from soil than the tree roots. As a result trees are often found growing on exceptionally poor soil simply because of the activities of the mycorrhizal fungus with which they are associated. Such a relationship is not uncommon among living organisms and is termed 'symbiosis'.

Examples of symbiosis

This is not the only example of symbiosis among fungi: there are many examples among the microscopic species, which ally themselves with green or blue-green algae to form lichens, perhaps the strangest of all organisms in the plant kingdom. There are fungi which live in symbiosis with insects (entomophilous fungi), in particular with cockroaches, termites and ants (myrmecophilous fungi). Such fungi live in the alimentary canal of the animals concerned and enable them to digest wood, paper and other such substances.

Among the various mycorrhizal fungi which are found in woods, there are some which associate with more than one tree species, while others are exclusive to one species. This is why, for example, the edible *Boletus edulis* occurs in oak woods, chestnut woods and pine woods, while *Boletus bovinus* occurs only beneath pines, and *Boletus elegans* only beneath larches. As a result, the species of tree is frequently the most important determining factor for symbiotic fungi.

It is worth knowing that there are also fungi living in mycorrhizal symbiosis with

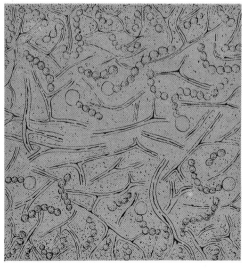

bushes and shrubs, and even herbaceous plants. The existence of healthy woodland is therefore vital for the life of many fungi, and vice versa. The preservation of forests and woodland is necessary not only to protect the trees themselves and safeguard the soil, but also for the sake of the many other organisms which are associated with these habitats.

In the same way it serves no purpose to trample on or otherwise destroy fungi which are not worth picking, or to destroy fungus mycelia. Even if these are of no use to us, they are useful to the wood, and specifically useful to those species of trees which need their symbiotic relationship. One should also remember that many small animals live on fungi, even the poisonous species. Snails

Above: The Field Mushroom in various stages of development, showing the ruptured veil
Left: Section of lichen tissue seen under a microscope. Many microscopic fungi form a close symbiotic relationship with algae to form a lichen. The chains of rounded cells belong to an alga, and the threads (hyphae) to a microscopic fungus

19

Right: A mycorrhiza seen under the microscope—the fungal hyphae form a mat (mycorrhiza) on the outside of the root and some of the hyphae can be seen penetrating the living root cells. A single root cell (above) shows the fungal hyphae coiled up within it

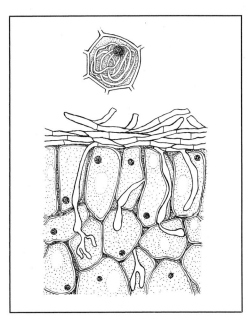

and slugs, numerous insects and their larvae, as well as apparently insignificant wood-dwelling creatures all depend on various fungi. In return, animals with sticky bodies, or small hairy feet become smeared with spores falling from the fungi and distribute them widely to start new mycelia. Prematurely destroyed fungi do not produce spores and, as a result, their chances of reproduction and propagation are reduced.

Parasitic species
Many of the larger fungi play a major role in woodlands because they are parasitic,

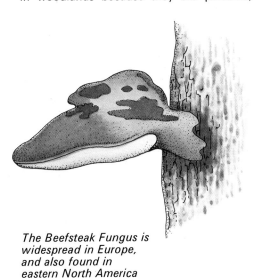

The Beefsteak Fungus is widespread in Europe, and also found in eastern North America

and some of these may, at a later stage, become saprophytic. Included in this group are those fungi which usually grow on living tree-trunks and gradually attack them by penetrating the wood itself. This causes the death of the tree, but the fungi can carry on growing and reproducing for as long as the wood from that tree can be used. In the end the tree is reduced to a state of spongy dryness, and the wood will have lost its characteristic structure. Many of the Polypores, or bracket fungi, and Agarics such as the Honey Fungus are in this category.

Among these fungi, there are species which live on almost any kind of tree—the Honey Fungus is one such example—while others grow only on one particular species of tree.

Other factors important in the determination of the fungus population are the type of soil, the altitude, the exposure of the land and the season of the year.

The soil, either sandy or chalky, gives a particular framework to the fungus population of a wood, and conspicuous differences may be observed between similar habitats. A beech wood, for example, growing in one type of soil will support a different group of fungus species from a beech wood on a different soil.

Geography and climate
Altitude greatly influences the habitat in which a fungus species will grow and this applies particularly to field species. There are striking differences between the fungus flora of lowland meadows and the species typical of mountain pastures. Seasonal differences are similarly marked in their effect on mushrooms and toadstools. Some species of fungus are found solely in the spring, others only in the summer, but most fungi appear in the autumn. There are also species which appear at any time of the year, except during severe winters. Instances also occur of fungi losing their strictly seasonal character and appearing 'out of turn'. This strange feature represents another of the many areas of study and research offered to mycologists. Rain, fog and mist, wind, dryness and temperature fluctuations tend to affect the numbers of individuals rather than the range of species, and they can often affect the appearance and colouring of fungi.

Fungi in the City

The fungi normally found in large towns and cities are not mycorrhizal and can survive without the existence of a symbiotic tree. Nevertheless, the presence of any tree is likely to encourage the persistence or new development of a mycorrhizal fungus and such fungi may suddenly make an unaccustomed appearance.

The Ink Caps

If the habitat offers soils with plenty of humus and organic matter, the fungus flora will include a wide variety of species, and the number of each species will gradually increase. A garden or orchard with fresh and fertile loam is an ideal habitat for numerous species of saprophytic fungi, particularly the short-lived species which sometimes appear one morning and are gone by the same evening. The so-called Common Ink Cap (*Coprinus atramentarius*) is one of the most astonishing fungi of all, because of the way it grows so quickly and perishes so soon. It sprouts from the ground almost without warning, in groups or clusters. At first its cap is ovoid that is, egg-shaped and pearl-grey or almost white in colour; then it becomes ochreous, striped with vertical flutes, and develops numerous small brownish scales on the uppermost part. The cap then becomes bell-shaped and when the fungus is fully grown (8–15 centimetres) it spreads out until it is almost flat-capped. It is a gilled fungus, with white gills turning greyish-pink, then grey-violet at the base. In the final stages, they turn dark, becoming completely black and dissolving into an inky liquid.

This black liquid is composed of numerous black spores, and is perfectly good for writing (hence the name of the fungus). The stalk is cylindrical, whitish, scaly in the lower part, and has a ring which drops off. The flesh of the young species is white and quite sweet. It is a gregarious fungus which likes chalky substrata. It grows from spring to autumn, and is especially abundant in the autumn after rain.

This species is edible if cooked when it is very young, but should not be eaten when larger. Like other *Coprinus* fungi, this species should never be consumed with alcohol.

The Shaggy Ink Cap or Lawyer's Wig (*Coprinus comatus*) is another fungus which causes the same reaction with alcohol, but which is equally harmless if taken without alcoholic drinks. It is in fact a mushroom delicacy. The species is so called because its cap, like that of *Coprinus atramentarius*, has numerous large scales on the outside which look like tresses of hair. White or cream-coloured, it is more fleshy than *Coprinus atramentarius*. The gills are white to begin with, turn pink at the base, then grey-violet and last of all black, but are less liquid in the final stages. The stalk is white and filled with a pithy or marrow-like substance, and has a movable ring. It grows in large clusters in gardens and orchards, and is particularly common along paths and on rubbish tips.

The genus *Coprinus* embraces a large number of species, including many which are small and fragile. A common species is the Glistening Ink Cap (*Coprinus micaceus*), found generally in dense clusters in woods and elsewhere where the soil has plenty of organic matter. It is five to ten centimetres high and has a flattened bell-shaped cap in the mature stage. This is ochre in colour and sprinkled with granules and small, bright scales—whence the name 'glistening'—which are arranged in vertical grooves. The stalk is slender, cylindrical and whitish; the gills are initially white, but turn purple-brown. The flesh is odourless, but bitter and is not edible.

The habitats chosen by Ink Caps are often shared by certain other, non-symbiotic fungi, also with distinctive shapes and giving off an extremely unpleasant smell. Particularly interesting are the Stinkhorn (*Phallus impudicus*) and *Clathrus cancellatus*.

Phallus impudicus (=*Ithyphallus impudicus*) belongs to the Gasteromycetes (family *Phallaceae*) and is egg-shaped in the early stages. It is also roughly the size of a chicken's egg, but is pink and soft to the touch, being contained in a membranous, pliable case.

As it develops, the 'egg' bursts and a cylindrical stalk emerges, 15–25 centimetres in height. The hollow stalk is white, delicate, pitted with numerous small 'dimples', and surmounted by a mitre-like cap, not unlike a Morel but perforated at the top. At first it is white, and then becomes covered by the gleba, a mucilaginous, greenish liquid which contains the spores. The Stinkhorn emits a smell which is somewhere between that of a carcass and the stench of garbage. This smell attracts swarms of flies, whose task of dispersing the spores is unwittingly carried out when their feet become smeared with the liquid from the cap. This species, one of the more curious of the summer fungi, is, in the opinion of some, edible when still at the egg stage.

The second species, *Clathrus cancellatus* (=*Clathrus ruber*), is even stranger. This inedible species also belongs to the Gasteromycetes (family *Clathraceae*) and is similarly egg-shaped and white when it emerges from the ground. As it develops and breaks out of its sheath, called an involucrum, which is soft, membranous and volva-like, a roundish and roughly-veined body appears. This is red outside and olive-coloured inside—the inside being clearly visible through the lattice-like structure of the fungus—the inside colour being the result of the spore-bearing gleba. The smell it gives off is even more unpleasant than that of the Stinkhorn.

Species of trees and shrubs

The array of fungi becomes larger and more intriguing if we consider a habitat like a large garden or park, where, as well as the humus in the soil and the presence of compost, there are also trees, shrubs, rockeries and lawns. This kind of urban habitat does make symbiotic alliances possible. For instance, Scots or White Pines are generally accompanied by pine-allied Boletes, and if the flowerbeds are ringed by stands of birch, then another kind of Bolete is often to be found. This is the species known variously as *Boletus leucophaeus* (=*Boletus scaber* = *Leccinum scabrum*) which lives in symbiosis with birches.

If a number of different trees are present, the likelihood of finding several associated fungi is greatly increased. There are five species commonly found under these conditions, all of them gilled: the Honey fungus and one of its close relatives; two poisonous fungi belonging to the *Hypholoma* genus and *Lyophyllum decastes*.

The Honey Fungus (*Armillaria mellea* = *Armillariella mellea*=*Clitocybe mellea*) is undoubtedly one of the commonest fungi of all. It is an autumnal species which grows

in clusters of anything up to ten individuals. It is to be found at the foot of numerous kinds of tree: Mulberry, False Acacia, and willows, poplars, oaks, pines and even shrubs such as blackcurrants. The colour of its cap varies somewhat with different host trees, this being a parasitic species which causes a great deal of damage. Its white felt-like mycelium is found beneath the bark, and causes the host tree to decay without any visible signs until, as happens occasionally, the tree starts to keel over. After a certain time—more than a year in some cases—the clusters of distinctive fungi appear.

Each young fruiting body has a cap which is initially conical-obtuse, that is, shaped like the head of a nail. It then becomes bell-shaped, with a central boss (umbo) like that of a shield, and finally almost flat with a diameter of 3–10 centimetres or slightly larger, and umbonate and rough in the upper part towards the middle. The younger fungi are darker and more vividly coloured, and turn gradually paler. Because of the variable colour of this species, indentification is sometimes difficult for the beginner. There

Above: The Common Ink Cap is commonly found growing in humus-rich soil

Above: This mature Stinkhorn shows clearly the ruptured egg and liquid spores
Above left: Coprinus picaceus specimens
Left: Clathrus cancellatus is one of the Stinkhorn group

are golden-yellow, brown, pale red and almost black varieties, but the commonest is reddish-ochre or honey-ochre, from which both the specific name *mellea* and the common name derive.

The stalk is cylindrical and slender, slightly swollen at the base, almost white in colour at the upper end and dark-reddish at the base. On the stalk, immediately beneath the cap there is a short-lived small ring, or *armilla* (hence *Armillaria*) which is white with a light yellow border. The gills are at first white, but soon become cream-coloured with red markings. This is in most circumstances an excellent edible mushroom, with white, firm flesh, but it should not be eaten immediately after a frost, and even less so if it has been sodden by rain. The stalks, which are fibrous and leathery, should be discarded.

The two poisonous species mentioned above belong to the genus *Hypholoma* (=*Nematoloma*). The first is the Sulphur-

Above: A clump of Honey Fungus newly emerged from dead or dying wood

Tuft (*Hypholoma fasciculare = Nematoloma fasciculare*), a fairly small mushroom, 5–12 centimetres in height, which also grows in clusters on old stumps where it can be found almost all year round. Its cap, 2–5 centimetres in diameter, is more convex, less umbonate, non-scaly, and varies from lemon-yellow to coppery-yellow, although at the centre the colour is darker or more orange; the gills are fairly close together, yellowish at first, turning to greyish-olive and eventually becoming bluish-violet. Its distinctive cap and dark spores make it readily identifiable. When the fungus is young it has a whitish-yellow fringe or frill which runs from the edge of the cap to the stalk, so affording protection to the gills, but this screen soon disappears. The stalk is cylindrical and slender, sometimes slightly undulating, sometimes curved in the lower part, the colour varying within the range of light yellows. The flesh is yellowish and bitter.

The second species is *Hypholoma sublateritium* (= *Nematoloma sublateritium*) which closely resembles the *fasciculare* species. It is, however, larger, reaching a height of 8–16 centimetres with a cap 3–10 centimetres in diameter, and is likewise

convex, non-umbonate and smooth. The colour is more intense than in the previous species, ranging from golden ochre-yellow on the edge, to orange or deep brick-red at the centre. The gills, to start with, are pale yellow, then progress through a brownish-olive green to become almost blackish-purple. The stalk is darker than in *Hypholoma fasciculare* and the flesh is slightly bitter. It grows in clusters but may also be found growing singly. Both this and the previous species are poisonous and may cause vomiting, colic pains, dysentery, and cold sweating.

Lyophyllum decastes (= *Tricholoma aggregatum* = *Clitocybe aggregata*) as the specific name implies, often grows in large and dense clusters. There are also related forms, such as *Lyophyllum connatum*, in which the stalks are connate, that is joined at the base. Each individual has an even or slightly wavy cap, convex or somewhat flattened, 5–12 centimetres in diameter, and brownish-grey in colour. Varieties occur which are more ash-grey as do some specimens which are coffee-coloured, and they invariably have distinctive darker coloured fibrous strands radiating from the

Above: Sulphur Tuft growing from rotting wood. The typical yellow and green colour is not fully developed

Left: Rhodophyllus sinuatus is a poisonous species
Below left: This is a clump of young Fairy Ring Mushrooms (Marasmius oreades), an edible species often used for seasoning

centre of the cap. The gills are very close together, being thin, slightly decurrent to the stalk, white at first and then subtly yellowish flesh-coloured.

This edible mushroom may easily be confused with the poisonous *Rhodophyllus sinuatus* (= *Entoloma lividum* = *Rhodophyllus lividus*), although this latter usually grows alone, is less evenly shaped and has deeper-coloured gills which are more widely separated. It is not hard to tell them apart if the spores are examined under the microscope, being transparent and oval in *Lyophyllum decastes,* and rose-coloured and angular in *Rhodophyllus*. The stalk of the latter is white and slightly swollen or curved in the lower part. The flesh is firm, white, sweet-tasting and not unlike the taste of raw vegetables.

The Fairy Ring Mushroom

Another very common mushroom found growing in an extremely wide variety of situations, and often on the grassy verges along busy roads, is the Fairy Ring Mushroom (*Marasmius oreades*). This is a small species, 5–12 centimetres in height, with a very slender, cylindrical, and hairy stalk which often tends to look rather contorted. The pale ochre-coloured stalk is surmounted by a thin cap, 3–5 centimetres in diameter, bell-shaped at first and brown-ochre, becoming wider with an umbo, and lighter ochre in colour. When mature, it tends to be slightly reddish if moist, and paler if dry. The gills are well separated, and usually 'free', that is completely free of the stalk. The flesh is tough, cream-coloured, pleasantly scented, sweet-tasting and good to eat. It is not a large fungus, but makes up for this by being plentiful. It is used as a seasoning for many dishes and can also be dried and kept without any difficulty.

For those who cannot tramp the fields or woods in search of wild mushrooms, a greenhouse can offer an ideal environment for the germination of certain species. Piles of compost, humidity and a temperature which never drops too low are all conducive to the growth of mushrooms.

Fungi of Fields and Meadows

Fields provide the typical habitat for a limited number of fungi. With the exception of a few species, these mushrooms are non-mycorrhizal, existing because of the presence of manure, or other organic matter.

Among the commonest of the fungi found in this habitat are a number of different field mushrooms. These are mushrooms in the normally accepted sense of the word, tending to grow to quite a large size, with a cylindrical stalk, which is sometimes slightly swollen at the base, without a volva and with a ring at the upper part of the stalk. The cap is even, ranging from spherical to hemispherical and eventually becoming virtually flat. It has gills on the lower side which are white or pink in the very young mushroom, and then become greyish-pink and violet and finally turn dark violet-brown and almost black in fully matured specimens.

Agaricus species

There is only one true Field Mushroom (*Agaricus campestris* = *Psalliota campestris*). The cap of the fully grown mushroom ranges from 5–10 centimetres in diameter, and sometimes more. It is white, greyish-white or brownish-white, sometimes smooth, and often covered with small darker scales which tend to be more numerous towards the centre of the cap. The stalk is white and has a white ring which eventually disappears. The gills are initially flesh-coloured, then violet-wine-coloured and almost black finally. The flesh is mostly white, but pale flesh-coloured near the gills and in the stalk. It has a fairly strong, distinctive smell, and a pleasant taste. This mushroom often grows in tight clusters or rings, from summer to autumn, anywhere from lowlands to mountain pastures.

A similar species is *Agaricus bisporus* (= *Psalliota bispora*), an edible mushroom which is now cultivated in numerous strains with a white, cream-coloured or brownish cap, sometimes smooth and sometimes thickly scaled. It is found growing wild in fields, meadows and also in the flowerbeds of parks and gardens where plenty of manure has been used.

Another allied species is the Horse Mushroom (*Agaricus arvensis* = *Psalliota arvensis*). It differs from *Agaricus campestris* in that it is slightly larger, with a cap up to 15–20 centimetres in diameter, which is less squat and whiter, with a hint of ochreous-grey at the centre. This species, which is also edible, has a more slender stalk than the Field Mushroom, with a full ring which looks as if it is double.

A common species of grassy places in summer and autumn, especially those near woods or forming clearings in woods, is the Wood Mushroom (*Agaricus silvicola* = *Psalliota silvicola*). This mushroom has a curious property; the cap, which is likewise white, with a hint of brown, and either smooth or scaly, tends to turn ochreous yellow if touched, as do the stalk, gills and flesh when in contact with the air; the flesh has a pleasant aniseed-like smell and is extremely palatable.

The way in which the flesh and skin of the cap turn yellow may cause this edible species to be confused with the Yellow-staining Mushroom (*Agaricus xanthodermus* = *Psalliota xanthoderma*) which is poisonous and can be distinguished by the unpleasant smell

Left: The Wood Mushroom (Agaricus silvicola)
Far Left: The Field Mushroom (Agaricus campestris)

and taste, and also by the way the flesh, especially of the stalk, instantly turns yellow at the slightest touch.

Lepiota species

Certain sorts of *Lepiota* will be found in fields and meadows, although they will also grow quite happily in the clearings of woods. One in particular, *Lepiota leucothites* (= *Lepiota naucina*), may be plentiful. This is a handsome fungus, 10–20 centimetres in height, with a cap 5–12 centimetres in diameter, spherical at first, then bell-shaped, and in full maturity almost flat, smooth, and silken-white. At the edge it sometimes retains a fringe, a remnant from the partial veil. This turns into a membranous ring, narrow and movable, near the top of the stalk. The stalk itself is slender and white, and the gills are also white to begin with, and then turn pale pink. The flesh, which is excellent to eat, is white and firm, with a subtle and pleasant smell and taste.

A related species is *Lepiota excoriata* (= *Macrolepiota excoriata*). It has more or less the same form and dimensions as *Lepiota leucothites,* but its gills are white in contrast to the pale brownish-ochre of *leucothites*. Its cap is also extremely scaly. It is good to eat, having white firm flesh, and is found occasionally in fields, heaths and near woods.

The same habitats are also host to the largest species of *Lepiota,* the Parasol Mushroom (*Lepiota procera* = *Macrolepiota procera*), which may grow to a height of 40 centimetres. Its cap, spherical to start with, becomes full and bell-shaped. Finally its magnificent cap is almost flat with a prominent umbo and measures 15–30 centimetres in diameter. The basic colour of this giant is brownish-white, with large brown scales covering it, particularly towards the centre where they are gathered thickly over the umbo.

In the young specimen the gills are white, turning light brownish-grey with various markings in the fully grown fungus. The stalk is hard and cylindrical, and swollen and bulb-shaped at the base. The surface of the cap displays much the same colours and features as the *leucothites* species, except that the scales are much more pronounced. High up on the stalk there is a narrow and very movable ring. The flesh is white and is

Above: The Yellow-staining Mushroom is a poisonous species similar to the Wood Mushroom
Right: Lepiota excoriata is one of the edible Lepiota species

edible, but the hard and extremely fibrous stalks should not be used.

Three species related to *Lepiota procera* have distinctive features which make them worthy of mention. The first, *Lepiota gracilenta*, is—as its name suggests—considerably more graceful than the *procera* species. It has a cap just 6—10 centimetres in diameter which is covered in scales like that of its larger relative, although these scales are smaller and more numerous. It grows in fields, meadows and on heaths, and is edible.

The second species is the Shaggy Parasol, (*Lepiota rhacodes*). This is generally smaller than *Lepiota procera*. The cap of the mature *rhacodes* specimen is less bell-shaped, rather flatter, and ends up being almost completely flat. It is covered with a brown outer layer or cuticle which shreds into wide, fibrillose scales. The stalk is less scaly and streaked, the gills showing reddish patches. The flesh also turns reddish when it comes in contact with the air.

Lepiota badhami (= *Leucocoprinus badhami*), the third of these species, is not unlike *Lepiota rhacodes* and *Lepiota procera*, but has a non-scaly stalk, a fixed ring, and colouring tending to purplish-brown. Its flesh also turns reddish when in contact with the air. This species is edible, but not particularly tasty.

There are many other species of *Lepiota*, among the larger species of which is *Lepiota friesii* (= *Lepiota acutesquamosa*). The latter specific name, meaning 'acute scales' derives from the cap which is thickly sprinkled with angular brown scales. Not all the *Lepiota* species are edible. *Lepiota cristata*, one of the smaller species, —only 3—8 centimetres in height—is poisonous. It has a bell-shaped cap 2—5 centimetres in diameter, initially white, with an umbo and small reddish-brown scales concentrically arranged. Later the cap becomes flattened with a distinctive umbo. The stalk is slightly swollen at the base, being white and slightly reddish at the bottom, with a fairly large, short-lived, white ring. It grows in fields, gardens and other cultivated places, as well as in woods.

Lepiota helveola is also poisonous. Its cap has a diameter of 3—6 centimetres, being convex to start with, then flattened, pinkish-ochre in colour, turning red when touched. Eventually the cap turns brown and cracked.

Above: This Parasol Mushroom clearly shows the warts on its cap and the movable ring
Left: Lepiota rhacodes, the aptly named Shaggy Parasol

The gills, however, are white and the stalk is lighter than the cap, with a ring which is short-lived and uneven. The flesh itself is white and tends to turn pink when in contact with the air. This species is also to be found in fields and meadows, in grassy places and in gardens, although it is comparatively rare.

The Morels

The preceding species all belong to the Basidiomycetes, but there are several larger Ascomycetes, collectively known as the Morels, which may also be found in grass or in the grassy clearings of woods. Apart from the distinctive nature of their spore-producing structures, the fruiting bodies of these fungi are very unusual in their shape. Their classification has provoked much argument among mycologists and the different opinions of the experts have led to some confusion. American and Continental mycologists have tended to split the various Morels into numerous species. British mycologists, however, tend to recognize only a few species in each of the main genera: *Morchella, Mitrophora, Verpa, Gyromitra* and *Helvella*. In countries where these fungi are common, they have been divided into many more species.

The genus *Morchella,* the True Morels, comprises only two species, *Morchella esculenta* and *Morchella elata.* Among those who enjoy eating fungi, the Common Morel (*Morchella esculenta = Morchella rotunda*) is highly sought after, not least because it appears in early spring, some time before other edible fungi emerge from the ground.

This Morel is often quite large, reaching a height of 25–30 centimetres; it has a, squat mitre-shaped and sometimes irregularly rounded cap. The cap's most distinctive features are its alveolae, or pits, which give this fungus its shrivelled, honeycombed appearance. Its ochre yellow colour becomes brown in the large pits and lighter white on the edges of the septa which form them. The stalk is white, hollow, swollen, unevenly cylindrical, and sometimes a little 'costate' or humped. This fungus sometimes grows in clusters, especially if the soil is sandy.

There is a smaller form of *Morchella esculenta* which is sometimes regarded as a separate species, *Morchella vulgaris.* The cap is again mitre-shaped, but more elongated

Above: Helvella crispa is an edible fungus with a convoluted cap (or mitre), and a fleshy, bulbous stalk

Left: Open broadleaf woods, such as this poplar wood, often contain grassy clearings or groundcover, where various grassland species can be found

and with smaller pits which are browner in colour; some specimens have earth-coloured or dark brownish grey caps. Like its relative, it is locally common in orchards, roadsides and under trees.

Morchella elata (= *Morchella conica*) is another edible species. In some countries it is dried and conserved on a commercial scale. It is small, and has a conical-tapering cap with narrow alveolae. These are brown in colour tending to blackish or olive-green, with parallel dividing ridges. This is not a common fungus and is mainly found in coniferous woodland.

Morchella semilibera is a slender species with a pointed, mitre-shaped cap, brown in colour with darker-coloured or black ribs. It differs from the other Morels in its cap. This is joined to the stalk internally and is completely free at its lower end whereas the stipe of *Morchella esculenta* is joined immediately to the lower edge of the cap. The stalk is white, cylindrical, and often slightly curved at the base. This species is edible, though less sought after than the preceding Morels, and is to be found in damp rich soil, usually in woods.

Mitrophora, Verpa and *Gyromitra* are other genera which belong to the Morels. The species of the genus *Verpa* can be clearly identified by their free cap, like that of *Morchella semilibera. Verpa* species, however, do not have a honeycombed cap. Instead it is smooth or pleated, in the shape of a bell, or a thimble. The stalk is elongated, cylindrical, white or slightly straw-yellow, slightly scaly and powdery, with the result that it presents numerous though barely perceptible ring-like swellings.

The main species is *Verpa conica*, which has a bell-shaped cap that is brown, and fluted-plicate, that is pleated. *Verpa digitaliformis,* somewhat smaller, with a thimble-like cap which is smoother and more ochreous or reddish, and sometimes even sepia-coloured, is sometimes regarded as a separate species. They are both edible and grow in gardens, along roadsides and even in woods.

The Turban Fungus

The genus *Gyromitra* is best represented by the Turban Fungus (*Gyromitra esculenta* = *Helvella esculenta*). This species has a spherical cap, reddish-brown or brown and even ochreous in colour, and is convoluted, rather like the contours of the human brain. The stalk is squat, whitish or slightly flesh-hued, powdery and hollow inside, as is the cap. The flesh is something like wax and has a good smell.

This fungus ranks highly among edible varieties, but must be well cooked. The Turban Fungus contains helvellic acid and so demands a certain amount of caution. This toxin is well-known because it is the probable cause of numerous cases of poisoning. It is especially harmful if swallowed repeatedly. The Turban Fungus is occasionally found in springtime in woods, and in particular near old pine stumps.

Gyromitra gigas is a very similar species which is larger and has a lighter-coloured cap. It is rare and found only in coniferous woods in continental Europe.

Helvellic acid, which is found in the Gyromitras and in certain Helvellas, acts according to the sensitivity of the individual concerned, indeed some people appear to be immune to it. Some experts claim that there is also a possibility of sensitization in people who eat these fungi for several days in succession, a practice which, for this reason alone, should be strictly avoided. Though it has been ascertained that helvellic acid is thermolabile—in other words, its toxicity is removed by cooking at a temperature of more than 60°C (140°F)—the toxicity of the Gyromitras persists at least in part, because helvellic acid seems to be associated with a substance which is capable of destroying the red blood corpuscles.

Helvella crispa

The species in the genus *Helvella,* the False Morels, are best represented by *Helvella crispa,* a curly-shaped autumnal Morel. It is quite a small species, 4–10 centimetres in height, with a thin, wavy cap. The cap is made distinctive by three upward-turned lobes which may either hang down over the stalk or be saddle-shaped. These lobes are ivory-white, straw-coloured or light-ochre and brighter on the lower surface and on the inside. The stalk is slightly swollen at the base and, like the cap, whitish or subtly ochreous. It is also markedly grooved and lacunose vertically, that is with sunken gaps. This autumnal Helvella is edible, but

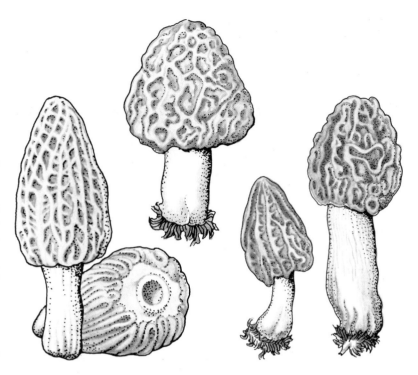

much less prized than the other Morels. Its flesh, white and wax-like in appearance and texture, is hard and elastic on the palate. This species is quite common in damp grassy places and in woods, and is rather similar to another species, *Helvella elastica,* which, however, has a stalk that is almost smooth and more slender.

A third species, not unlike the above, is *Helvella lacunosa;* its cap is more unevenly 'lobate' with three flatter lobes, black or blackish-grey-brown in colour on both surfaces. The stalk, slightly paler than the cap, is very like that of *Helvella crispa* with the same grooves and distinctive vertical lacunae which, if anything, are even more marked in this species.

This group also includes *Helvella monachella;* it is so named because it has a cap which is blackish-brown on its upper surface and pale below and inside the lobes. The stipe is whitish, unevenly cylindrical, and neither grooved nor lacunose. It is edible, though not particularly tasty, and may be found in spring in grassy woods and gardens.

This species is not found in Britain, however, nor is *Helvella infula,* a fungus with a trilobate cap, brownish-red or even terracotta in colour, and velvety in texture. The whitish, powdery-looking stalk has vertical lacunae and hollows, and is reddish in colour. It grows in woods during the summer and autumn, and is edible. Its general appearance is somewhat reminiscent of *Gyromitra esculenta.*

Above: (left to right) Morchella elata, Morchella esculenta and Mitrophora hybrida. The last species is not found in Britain

Fungi of Broadleaf Woods

Since fungi are unable to make their own food, they depend either on decaying organic material such as wood, leaves and excreta or on other living organisms. In the latter case they will exist as parasites or in symbiosis with a tree. Of all the possible habitats which provide these varied food sources, woodland offers by far the richest environment.

Some fungi, such as *Paxillus involutus*, are found in a wide variety of both broadleaf and coniferous woods. This *Paxillus* species may be found growing beside woodland glades and streams, and is sometimes known as the Brown Chantarelle because it somewhat resembles the Chantarelle in appearance. It is a fungus fairly common in summer and autumn, with a short stalk and a flat cap which eventually becomes slightly depressed, that is, concave, or funnel-shaped, and is dark-ochre to bluish-brown in colour. The gills, however, are often

Above: Pholiota aegerita is one of the edible tree fungi

Previous page: The scaly Pholiota squarrosa (top) juts from the base of a dead tree. Paxillus involutus (bottom) is another woodland species; recognizable by its inrolled cap margin and eccentric stalk

lighter and its colour tends to deepen if touched. The specific name *involutus* derives from the fact that the edge of the cap is involute, that is, curls slightly over the gills, which extend some way down the stalk (decurrent). The flesh, reddish-yellow or olive-coloured, is edible when cooked and may be dried, but altogether it is not a very enticing fungus.

Another common fungus found in woods generally is the Clouded Clitocybe (*Clitocybe nebularis*). This handsome, rather squat fungus, with a cap 8–15 centimetres in diameter, is convex with an umbo and in the latter stages almost flat and even depressed. Normally ash-grey in colour, the cap may sometimes occur more whitish or tending to brownish or light chamois-coloured, and has a distinctive rim when young. The gills are very close together, white at first and then ivory and slightly decurrent to the white or pearl-grey stalk. The stalk itself is slightly swollen at the base which is covered with a white down. The flesh is white, and has a typical mushroom smell, or may smell of flour. The taste of this autumnal species is slightly acrid, but it is strictly speaking edible when cooked and may also be dried. However, its taste is definitely one that needs acquiring, and some disagreement about its edibility persists; some authors consider it inedible, while others find it excellent.

There are relatively few fungi found both in woodland and grassy habitats. One of these is the St. George's Mushroom (*Tricholoma gambosum*). It has a thick cap, ranging from white or straw-coloured to greyish-brown, and is a fine velvet in texture. Convex at first, it becomes progressively flatter as it grows and may be finally completely flat. It is usually slightly umbonate, with a tightly curled edge. The gills are very close together and white, while the white stalk is thick, sometimes slightly bulging or swollen at the base. The flesh is white too, and firm, emitting a strong smell of flour. This is an edible fungus found between spring and summer which grows in lines or rings, called 'fairy rings' after the suddenness with which they spring up.

Another group found on the edge of woods are the Entolomas (*Rhodophyllus* species), a large genus with salmon-coloured spores. Among these are *Rhodophyllus sinuatus,* a species of open broadleaf woods, which has a cap 7–12 centimetres in diameter and greyish-ochre in colour, with a curved, whitish stalk. *Rhodophyllus staurosporus* is a small species commonly found in grass and woody clearings. The cap is only 2–4 centimetres in diameter, brown in colour and convex in shape. An occasional species is *Rhodophyllus dichrous*, a slightly larger species which is found along wood margins. It has an umbonate, grey-brown cap and scaly, violet-grey stalk. Of all the *Rhodophyllus* species, perhaps the most distinctive to the casual, unwitting passer-by will be *Rhodophyllus nidorosus,* which has an extremely noticeable nitrous smell.

Pholiota species

The species described so far have been soil-dwelling, existing on buried material or in symbiosis with living tree roots. A great many woodland fungi are, however, parasitic. One of the most unusual examples is that of *Sclerotinia tuberosa,* which lives on the underground stems of the Wood Anemone (*Anemone tuberosa*). The destructive effect of some of these parasitic fungi may be marked. One of the worst is the Honey Fungus (*Armillaria mellea*) which attacks an enormous range of trees and shrubs. The aptly named *Pholiota destruens* is another such species. It has a cap 5–20 centimetres in diameter, and is ochre or bistre in colour. Numerous pale-coloured tufts are conspicuous in young specimens, and the gills are often slightly decurrent, whitish at first and later russet-ochre. The stalk is slightly larger than in the Honey Fungus, slightly curved at the base, and scaly, while the ring is short-lived and off-white. The flesh itself is white and has an unpleasant taste and smell. This formidable fungus is a particular parasite of poplars.

Other *Pholiotas,* however, are not parasitic. *Pholiota squarrosa* grows on bark, being a so-called corticolous species, and is found on a wide range of trees. Like many *Pholiota* species, it grows in small clumps. Its cap and stalk are covered with large brownish-yellow fluffy scales on a reddish-yellow background, but the stalk is smooth above the ring. Although the flesh is yellow and smells of rotting wood, it is edible when cooked. However, it is important that the water used for the initial boiling is thrown away, and must not be used for cooking other food.

Pholiota praecox (= *Agrocybe praecox*) is smaller than the other *Pholiota* species mentioned. It occurs in the spring or early summer and has a slightly umbonate, brownish or straw-coloured cap. The gills are close together, whitish-grey in young specimens and later russet-ochre. The stalk

is long, slender, off-white, slightly swollen at the base and in the upper part has a pendulous, short-lived ring. The flesh is sweetish and smells of flour. In the opinion of many gatherers, it is an excellent, edible fungus and is widely eaten in some countries. Its usual habitat is deciduous woods and pastures.

Pholiota aegerita (= *Pholiota cylindracea* = *Agrocybe cylindracea*) grows on the trunks and stumps of poplars and other trees between the spring and autumn. It has a hemispherical cap which eventually becomes almost flat, and reaches a diameter of 10–12 centimetres. The colour of this species varies from dark brown when young to a tawny or honey shade, and may be almost white. The gills are whitish at first, and then take on the ochre colour of the spores. The stalk is firm, cylindrical, smooth, white or almost white, and in the upper part has a wide ring which is also white. The white flesh has a pleasant taste and smell, and makes this an excellent fungus for the table, especially if it is picked when still young. Because it is not a mycorrhizal species, it has the added virtue of being easy to cultivate on blocks of poplar wood buried in the ground and kept moist.

Pholiota mutabilis is a species which grows in large clusters on tree-stumps and tree-trunks, and may be found from spring

Above: Woodlands are frequently very varied in their composition and hence, their fungal flora. Even this narrow belt of trees by a river will support a number of interesting species

almost right through to winter. The cap is initially hemispherical, but becomes progressively less domed, and in maturity is almost flat. It ranges in colour from yellow to cinnamon, being slightly darker at the centre where there is often a small umbo. The slightly decurrent gills range from yellowish to ochreous and are hidden for some time by the whitish partial veil, which joins the edge of the cap to the stalk. The stalk has the same colouring as the cap, although the top is lighter and is scaly up to the short-lived ring at its upper end. The flesh, ranging from whitish to yellow in colour, emits a pleasant mushroom smell and has an excellent taste. This edible fungus, apart from being a good ingredient for stews, can also be dried.

Another small fungus which may abound in such habitats is *Collybia velutipes* (= *Flammulina velutipes*), a fungus which grows in thick clusters on stumps and even on old posts or stakes, and is especially common in autumn and winter. Its cap 3–8 centimetres in diameter is slimy, tawny-yellow, becoming darker-coloured at a later stage. The stalk is cylindrical, slightly curved at the base, sometimes eccentric, and pale yellow at the top changing to a velvety dark-brown in the lower half. The flesh is yellowish, only faintly scented and although bitter, edible. However, it must be well cooked to remove the bitter taste.

Bracket fungi
On the larger trunks of woodland trees numerous types of bracket fungi may be found. Among them, the Oyster Fungus (*Pleurotus ostreatus*) is a common species. It has a wide cap, almost shell-shaped, wavy at the edge, greyish sepia-brown in colour, though sometimes very pale-coloured. The whitish gills are fairly separate, decurrent to the stalk. This is invariably eccentric (not centrally placed), and is at some times clearly visible, and at others virtually non-existent. It is edible when young and, furthermore may be found throughout the year. It is, however, a parasitic species and causes considerable damage on many trees, especially beech. The closely related *Pleurotus columbinus*, which is considered by many to be a variety of the *ostreatus* species usually has a larger stalk, together with a distinctive leaden-grey to dark blue-violet

Above: This parasite, the Oyster Fungus, shows its widely separated gills Right: It is a familiar edible species and causes considerable damage on beech trees

Left: Clitocybe nebularis despite its excellent taste, may be indigestible Above left: The St George's Mushroom has deserved renown as an edible species

cap. These two fungi are widely cultivated in Italy.

Similar species are the Elm Fungus (*Pleurotus ulmarius*) and *Pleurotus cornucopiae*. The former grows on elms and is a large white fungus which is edible when young. Its flesh, which is also white, is slightly acid and requires a certain amount of cooking before it is fit to be eaten. *Pleurotus cornucopiae* is a summer species and grows in conspicuous clusters on old oak and other broadleaf trunks. It has a fleshy cap, convex at first, becoming concave with a deep funnel. The cap is slightly uneven in shape and whitish with an ochre-coloured shading which is more visible in fully grown specimens. The gills are very decurrent, extending a long way down the stalk and eventually becoming interwoven to form a reticulum or network. White or pale flesh-coloured, they follow the shape of the cap, which itself tapers to a cone as

it merges with the stalk. The stalk is whitish and downy, usually eccentric and curved. The flesh, which is fairly spongy to the touch, is white and smells of flour.

The Polypores are another important group of bracket fungi. One of the commonest, which is found from spring right through autumn on the large trunks of many broadleaf trees, including willows, poplars, plane-trees and maples, is the Dryad's Saddle Fungus (*Polyporus squamosus* = *Polyporellus squamosus*). Its large shelf-like caps, either flat or slightly concave and fan-shaped, may reach a radius of 40–50 centimetres. The caps of this curious species grow on short stalks, with a squat and eccentric foot. They are usually straw-coloured above, although brownish-ochre specimens may occur, with sparse but large dark-brown scales. Below, the cap is whitish, turning yellowish, and completely and subtly riddled with small holes because of the presence of the pores. The tubules are white and decurrent to the stalk, which is blackish and velvety at the base. The flesh is white, firm and well-textured, with a strong smell of acid flour. Some care must be taken with this species; it can only be eaten when very young, and must be cooked first.

Another handsome Polypore of similar dimensions and equally imposing appearance is *Polyporus sulphureus* (= *Laetiporus sulphureus*). It has a radius of 30–40 centimetres and is common on broadleaved trees, especially oak, willow and cherry, and also on conifers, in summer and autumn. This species often has numerous sessile caps— that is, caps which are stalkless, rising straight from the surface on which they are growing. These are superimposed and joined together, in the shape of uneven brackets or shelves, and lobed along the free edge. The colour of the upper face ranges from sulphur-yellow to very bright reddish-orange, but the edge is often lighter, with less brightly-coloured patches. Below, the caps are light sulphur-yellow with very small pores. The flesh is whitish or pale yellow, slightly acid, and in older specimens somewhat bitter. This species is only edible when the fungi are young and is considered to have no culinary value. It is noticeably hard to digest because the flesh is often leathery.

Above: Grifola sulphurea is found on wood in summer and autumn
Left: A typical view of this beautiful but destructive fungus

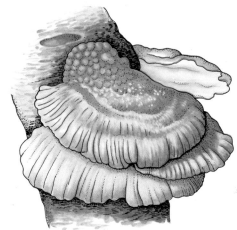

Corticolous fungi

There are many corticolous fungi which are completely leathery, corky or woody. Of these the *Ganoderma*, *Fomes* and *Piptoporus* genera are fairly common. Another example is *Daedalea quercina*, which frequently occurs on old tree-trunks. The fruit-bearing bodies are hoof-shaped, 5–30 centimetres across, with the texture of cork. They are homogenously grey, bistre or brownish in colour, smooth and slightly wavy on the top, with wide, elongated or quite rounded labyrinthine pores below. This species is, of course, not edible.

The so-called Jew's Ear fungus (*Auricularia auricula* = *Hirneola auricula*) is a corticolous fungus of 3–10 centimetres diameter. This species grows in clusters all year round on the trunks of old elder bushes and very occasionally on other genera such as *Buddleia* and *Robinia*. This unusual member of the Basidiomycetes belongs to a group of Jelly Fungi (*Tremellales*). It has an

Opposite page: Polyporus squamosus is another 'bracket' fungus which grows on dead trees. It is quite common in spring and edible when young

elastic and gelatinous consistency and ear-like shape, and is unevenly lobed; the concave part contains the fertile layer (hymenium) and is grooved and veined. The colour varies with age and the weather, being ochre, dark brown-red or flesh-coloured. It is edible but cannot be said to be anything more than very mediocre in quality. According to some authors it is a laxative.

The Amanitas

Among the most widely-distributed of fungus genera and found in many types of woodland are the Amanitas. These are Basidiomycetes with caps. Their gills are usually white, as are their spores. They have a central stalk typically contained at the base in a sort of pouch called the volva, but often reduced to a mere ledge or a few cottony scales. Another common feature, with only rare exceptions, is the conspicuous skirt-like ring which occurs at the top of the stalk and drops down over the stalk.

The most famous *Amanita* is the Death Cap, (*Amanita phalloides*). Its notoriety stems from the simple fact that it is the most poisonous fungus known. This species is 10–20 centimetres in height, and its cap is initially rounded, but becomes convex and finally flat. The cap is 3–14 centimetres in diameter and very variable in colour, ranging from light olive-green to darker shades, and from olive-yellow to lemon-yellow to almost ivory-white. It is in general slightly darker at the centre, with very thin and darker radial fibrils or strands. This colour variation may cause a confusion to the beginner which he can ill afford.

In rare cases it is possible to see traces of the volva on the cap, although such traces are typical of other related species. The volva itself is white and bulbous, and the gills are white and close together. The white stipe is cylindrical and slightly bulbous at the base. It is also slightly marbled and has a very conspicuous white ring at the top. The flesh is white and firm, and those unfortunates who eat it discover that it has not much taste or smell. What smell there is, is mushroomy and unpleasant, and may become somewhat foetid.

Poisoning from the Death Cap is extremely serious; the first symptoms appear between 10 and 30 hours after swallowing the fungus (seldom after six to eight hours or 48 hours),

when the victim has more or less discounted any such possibility. Even a very small portion can prove fatal. The poison affects the liver, kidneys, and the heart muscle. The first signs of poisoning are given by the digestive system and then further confirmation is offered by the sufferer's state of general and serious weakness, which can often end in death. Modern treatments offer some hope of survival, and include filtering the blood through charcoal. This gruesome species grows in many kinds of broadleaf woods (oak woods most of all), and sometimes in coniferous woods, from summer to autumn.

Two other closely related species are *Amanita verna* and *Amanita virosa*. The first is completely white, with the cap straw-coloured, if at all, at the centre and the

Above: There are many colour forms of the lethal Death Cap, which may make it difficult for the beginner to identify

Opposite page: An oak wood is one of the richest habitats for fungi. Many contain other tree species which widen the range of fungi present. They are relatively light and support many groundcover plants

*Above: Chestnut woods
are a typical habitat for
the Death Cap
Below right: The
greenish form of the
Death Cap at various
stages of development*

stalk powdery above the ring. It grows from spring until autumn, despite its specific name, *verna* meaning spring, and is to be found in the calcareous soil of broadleaf woodland, especially oak woods.

Amanita virosa, known as the Destroying Angel, is white, and differs from *Amanita verna* in that its cap is more bell-shaped, at least initially. Its stalk is generally downy above the ring and very marbled lower down. It prefers woodlands and sandy soil. Both these species are lethal, like the Death Cap.

All these deadly species can be distinguished from the edible mushrooms by their white gills and the presence of a volva; mushrooms have grey, pink or chocolate gills and no volva. Despite such distinguishing features, the collector may often be in doubt, and should never gather a species unless certain of its identity and characteristics.

There are a few Amanitas which do not have a ring. Among them is *Amanita vaginata* (= *Amanitopsis vaginata*) which has the same general shape as the Death Cap. However, its cap, which is 4—15

slightly depressed. The cap may reach 15–20 centimetres in diameter, the gills are white or faintly straw-coloured, and the stalk and ring are white. The volva does not retain its pouch-like shape but breaks up into warts. Some of these remain on the surface of the cap and others around the base of the mushroom, which is swollen with a scaly appearance. The flesh is mostly white, although reddish-yellow beneath the outer layer of the cap, firm and has no distinctive smell.

There are numerous known varieties of this species and one can mention just two which are perhaps the most important: var. *regalis,* with a darker cap, and var. *aureola,* which has a wartless cap. Although the warts are a distinctive feature of *Amanita muscaria,* they may, incidentally, be washed off the cap by heavy and prolonged rain.

Amanita muscaria appears in the autumn, often in large numbers, in broadleaf or mixed woods, preferring stands of birch and fir. This species and all its varieties are poisonous, but there are many devotees who maintain that when the epidermis (skin) of the cap is removed, and thus the warts as well, these mushrooms may be boiled and safely eaten. Indeed, in certain markets in Southern Russia, *Amanita muscaria* is sold over the counter. It may be that there are certain regional strains of the species which are not poisonous, or at least far less toxic. One thing is certain, it is much less dangerous than *Amanita phalloides,* but it can cause an 'atropine-muscarine' syndrome. The symptoms of poisoning appear earlier and less violently than in the case of the Death Cap, and consumption is seldom fatal. Its specific name 'muscaria' refers to its use in bygone days as a fly-killer.

A more dangerous, often lethal, species is the Panther (*Amanita pantherina*), which also contains the poison muscarine. It is smaller than *Amanita muscaria,* its cap being 6–8 centimetres in diameter. The cap is grey-brown or brown in colour, marginally striated and warted and, unlike the species mentioned above, the cap is not flat, but more pyramidal. When young it is egg-shaped, like *Amanita muscaria.* It is slightly narrower half way up, so that one can identify the part which will become the cap, and the part which will form the stalk, which

centimetres in diameter, is a different colour, ranging from light grey to the lead colour of the var. *plumbea* form. The cap is conspicuously striate, that is, marked with thin lines, at the edge and slightly umbonate at the centre. The stalk is white but not marbled and the volva is more tubular, in other words comparatively narrower and taller. A variety of this species is the Tawny Grisette (*Amanita fulva*), whose cap varies in colour from red-brown to tawny. There is also another less common variety with a white cap (var. *alba*). The flesh of this fungus is white and has a pleasant smell and taste. *Amanita vaginata* is to be found from summer to autumn in woods, particularly beech, in heathland and even in meadows. It is edible, like *Amanita fulva.*

The Fly Agaric, another famous Amanita, (*Amanita muscaria*) has a red cap—more accurately, orange in fully grown specimens—with the upper surface dotted with what look like white warts, and are actually remnants of the volva.

In shape it is at first spherical, then convex, and finally flat with an umbo, or

Above: Amanita vaginata is an edible species not to be confused with the lethal Amanitas
Below: The lethal Amanita verna resembles the harmless species vaginata

remains swollen and has an adherent, pronounced volva with small swellings. Gills, stalk and ring are white. The firm, white flesh has a wine-like smell, especially in older specimens. It grows from summer to autumn in broadleaf woods, coniferous woods and on heaths, especially near beech.

The Panther is sometimes confused with the Blusher (*Amanita rubescens*) and with *Amanita excelsa*. The former tends to be completely suffused with a winy-reddish colour, especially in certain varieties. The cap is not striate at the edge and has grey warts, while the ring is large and membranous, but the volva hardly visible. The flesh is white but turns wine-red when in contact with the air. Poisonous if eaten raw, it is an edible fungus when cooked, because cooking destroys the haemolytic poison which

Above: Amanita ceasarea is a handsome and highly favoured European species not found in Britain

Left: The fruiting body breaks out of the typical Amanita 'egg' Opposite page: The Fly Agaric is the fairytale toadstool (above). This poisonous species begins as an innocuous-looking white 'egg' (bottom)

it contains. It grows in mixed woods during summer and autumn.

Amanita excelsa is rather stockier than *Amanita pantherina,* with a more ash-grey cap and powdery-whitish warts. The stalk is conspicuously striate at the top, while the volva is reduced to brownish markings. *Amanita aspera,* with an olive-ochre to greyish-bistre cap, very much resembles the edible *Amanita excelsa.*

Other Amanitas which grow in broadleaf or mixed woods are *Amanita porphyria, Amanita junquillea* (= *Amanita gemmata*), *Amanita citrina* (= *Amanita mappa*) and *Amanita solitaria* (= *Amanita strobiliformis*). The first species is uncommon and more typically found in coniferous woods during autumn. It is not poisonous but its flesh has an unpleasant smell, which makes eating it inadvisable. It has a brownish cap, tending sometimes to be wine- or violet-coloured, and has none of the characteristic striations. The gills and stalk are white with a short-lived ring which is white above, brown below. The volva, like a whitish pouch, is free at the edge and entire, which enables a distinction to be made between this species and *Amanita pantherina,* the volva of which has superimposed swellings.

The rare *Amanita junquillea* (= *Amanita gemmata*), a jonquil-coloured species, has a cap the colour of which varies from golden-yellow to reddish-yellow, with a striated edge. The colour sometimes tends to be ochreous and may even be much darker, which could cause this species to be muddled with the Panther. It is thus advisable not to consider eating this mushroom.

Amanita citrina (= *Amanita mappa*), the False Death Cap, has a pale yellow cap, as its specific name suggests and is also found in a white form, var. *alba.* The surface of the cap is covered at random with brightly-coloured shreds of the overall veil; the gills are white or faintly pale yellow, and close together. The stalk is the same colour, bulbous at the base, with the volva free at the edge. The flesh itself is white or tending slightly to yellow beneath the cuticle or outer layers of the cap, and emits an unpleasant smell of raw root vegetables. This inedible species grows in autumn in broadleaf and coniferous woods. This, too, may be confused with poisonous species such as *Amanita phalloides* and *Amanita virosa.*

Above: This is a completely red form of the Fly Agaric, called var. aureola
Left: Birch woods occur on light sandy soil. The Fly Agaric is one of the commonest fungi of this type of woodland

The edible *Amanita solitaria* is completely white, or may, exceptionally, have a slightly greyish or ochreous cap, particularly at the centre. The warts are pale-grey, truncated and pyramidal or flattened. The volva is formed by a short-lived layer of powdery scales and the ring is also downy and short-lived. This is a fairly rare mushroom which may be found in summer and autumn in sunny woods and thickets.

The Boletes

Another large, well-known group of fungi to be found in the woods are the Boletes. These have a central stipe with a fleshy cap whose lower surface is composed of vast numbers of pores and fine tubules. At the top of the stalk, many Boletes have a fine reticulum (or honeycomb). Some, at least when young, have a white, membranous veil, termed a partial veil, which protects the pores and gradually disappears as the mushroom develops, becoming a short-lived ring on the upper part of the stalk. At one time, the Boletes were associated with the Polypores, but their true affinity is with the Agarics. With one exception, Boletes are soil-dwelling fungi, whereas Polypores usually grow on wood. The tubules of Boletes may also be removed cleanly from the flesh, which is not possible with Polypores.

Most Boletes are edible; exceptions are *Boletus satanas* and the Boletes in the *Boletus pustureus* group. As a general rule it is best to avoid Boletes with red pores, even though they may turn out to be quite

Above: The Panther is a very poisonous Amanita species
Below: The Panther breaks out to form the distinctive, warty Amanita fruiting body

Above: Three specimens of Amanita rubescens. The flesh of the Blusher is edible when cooked and turns reddish if damaged

harmless species, at least when cooked.

The best-known Bolete is the Cep (*Boletus edulis*), and the most sought-after by mushroom gatherers. It is prized because it is harmless raw or cooked and because of its exquisite flavour. It has a convex cap which becomes flattened and varies considerably in colour from light ochre to grey-brown or dark chestnut. The pores change from white, to yellowish and then to an olive colour. The stalk may be squat or tapered and is lighter than the cap, sometimes occurring almost white with brownish patches. At the top, the stalk has a fine reticulum. There are varieties which are almost white, var. *albus,* and there is one pale yellow variety, var. *citrinus.* It grows in oak and chestnut woods, but also often abounds among firs.

Closely related and similar is the Summer Cep (*Boletus edulis* ssp. *reticulatus* = *Boletus aestivalis* = *Tubiporus reticulatus*), which favours woods composed of chestnut, oak, hornbeam, birch or beech. Whereas the preceding species is more typically autumnal, this is a principally summer mushroom. As well as differing seasonally, it is particularly identifiable by its reticulum, which covers the stalk almost to the base, unlike the Cep where it is only found at the top.

Two other types of Cep are worthy of mention. The first is *Boletus aereus,* a distinctive species because it is squat and has a dark-brown to blackish-brown cap. The pores are white, then olive-yellow. The stalk is short and thick, considerably broader in the middle, ochreous to brownish in colour, with the reticulum initially light-coloured, becoming brown as the fungus matures. This excellent-tasting species likes

oak and chestnut woods and is also found
in beech woods.

In the three Boletes mentioned above, the
flesh is firm—especially in the case of *Boletus
aereus*—and is white or possibly slightly
coloured beneath the cuticle of the cap.

The other species of Cep, *Boletus pinicola*
(= *Tubiporus pinicola* = *Boletus edulis
pinicola*) is more typical of woods composed
of Scots Pines and Norway Spruces. The
cap of this extremely tasty fungus tends to
be coppery red and is viscous when the
weather is damp. The pores are white, then
pale yellow, and finally olive-coloured, while
the stalk is brownish or reddish with a
conspicuous white or pale brown reticulum.
The flesh is reddish beneath the cuticle of the
cap.

In its juvenile stage, another similar
Bolete, *Boletus felleus* (= *Tylopilus felleus*)

*Above: Amanita citrina
is a non-poisonous
species which has a
disagreeable smell of
raw potatoes
Left: The highly-prized
Cep is a typical Bolete
with no ring or volva
and a spongy mass of
spores beneath the cap*

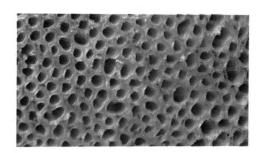

Above: Another edible Bolete, Boletus aereus, shows the typical squatness of the genus and has pores like those of the Cep which are shown under magnification (top)

Opposite page: The edible Boletus pinicola is sometimes regarded as a form of the Cep

may be muddled with the tasty Cep. The shape closely resembles the Cep and the colouring is also quite similar. However, the cap is different, more olive-coloured, and the stalk tends to be of a less warm colour. The reticulum is dark, with rather elongated meshes, and reaches to the bottom of the stalk. It can be easily distinguished from the real Cep by its tubules, which are initially pinkish-white and develop into a dirty, more pronounced grey-pink colour. The flesh is white and firm, but extremely bitter, which makes it quite inedible, although it is not actually poisonous.

The remaining Boletes form a fairly limited group. Mention has already been made of them in the form of *Boletus leucophaeus* (= *Leccinum scabrum*) which is symbiotic with birch trees. This and related fungi are sometimes distinguished as two major species; *Boletus scaber,* which is grey, and *Boletus rufus* (*Leccinum versipelle*) which is reddish. Academically speaking, the species are more numerous than this and include the following: *Boletus carpini, Boletus leucophaeus, Boletus duriusculus* and *Boletus aurantiacus,* all of which are edible, even though their flesh turns black when cooked. For simplicity, some mycologists lump the species together, while others split them into numerous species.

The first species, *Boletus carpini,* may be lumped with the 'grey' Boletus, that is, with the true *Boletus scaber.* Its cap is 5–12

Above: Boletus carpini turns black when cooked
Below right: Boletus felleus is found in a wide range of woods and has a bitter taste

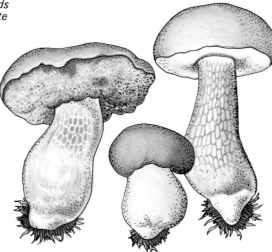

centimetres in diameter, hemispherical at first, but almost flat in mature specimens, very fleshy, from grey-brown to grey-ochre in colour and sometimes very light-coloured. The pores are faintly greyish with yellowish shading. The stalk is quite slender, thin at the top, often slightly curved, and covered with a fairly scaly rough layer, which is blackish-grey in colour, with longitudinal markings. The flesh is whitish, passing to violet and then to grey. It is a rare species of broadleaf woods, especially under hornbeam and hazel.

Boletus leucophaeus (= *Leccinum scabrum*) has a cap which tends to be pale chestnut-brown. The pores are white and turn pinkish while the blackish granulations of the stalk are more irregular. The flesh is white and more or less unchanging. This species grows almost exclusively beneath birch trees.

Boletus duriusculus is much more robust, with a brown cap and a stalk which has a reticulum at the top, usually with bluish markings. The flesh becomes violet-pink when cut and the species is to be found growing mainly in the vicinity of poplars.

Boletus aurantiacus (= *Leccinum aurantiacum* = *Krombholzia aurantiaca*), which is sometimes called the Red Boletus, is a sturdier species than the preceding ones, and differs from them mainly by having a brick-coloured or more orange-reddish cap. The pores of this species, which prefers chestnut woods, are white and then grey-ochre. The stalk is covered with rough white patches of down in the young specimen, which then turn orange-ochre and finally dark brown—these patches are blackish in the related *Boletus rufescens.* The flesh is white and becomes blackish-violet with bluish patches when cut.

There are two rare edible Boletes which are distinctive because their stalks are almost completely hollow or contain in the inner cavity septa or strips of pithy flesh.

The first is *Boletus castaneus* (= *Gyroporus castaneus*), a small species, with a hemispherical cap which in older growths becomes almost flat and is chestnut-coloured. Its pores are white and turn slightly yellowish and the stalk of the young fungus is solid, but soon becomes hollow. Externally the stalk is the same colour as the cap, and lighter at the top. The flesh is white, unchanging in colour, and has a pleasant taste. It is a rare species of both broadleaf and coniferous woods and found from the summer to autumn months.

The second species is *Boletus cyanescens* (= *Gyroporus cyanescens*) which is larger than the preceding species, with an ochre-olive cap, white turning to ivory-coloured

Above: Boletus rufus in various stages of development. The granulations on the stalk are an important feature in distinguishing various Boletes
Above left: Boletus scaber is an edible species, closely allied to Boletus carpini

pores, and becomes patched with blue when touched. The stalk, which is thin at the top, is lighter in colour than the cap. The flesh is white, but disconcertingly turns deep blue on cutting. Despite these colour changes, it is not only edible but a very tasty species.

Now we come to a group of Boletes in which the caps are predominantly brown, with predominantly yellow solid stalks. The pores are either small and round or larger and angular depending on the species. They are invariably yellow in the young fungus, and olive-coloured in fully grown specimens.

Of these species, *Boletus subtomentosus* (= *Xerocomus subtomentosus*) has a slightly velvety cap, the colour of which passes from bistre to reddish-brown, often with olive-coloured shades. The stalk is yellow with longitudinal and often conjoined ribs which are red-brown in colour. The flesh is mainly yellow, but slightly reddish beneath the cuticle of the cap and becomes greenish-blue when exposed to the air. It is edible and grows between summer and autumn in chestnut and beech woods.

A very similar species is *Boletus chrysenteron* (= *Xerocomus chrysenteron*), which is generally slightly smaller, with a cap which becomes quickly cracked. The pores are larger and the stalk has lighter-coloured streaks which are not amalgamated. The flesh of this species is also more reddish beneath the cuticle of the cap, and it grows in oak woods, birch woods and beech woods.

Boletus badius (= *Xerocomus badius*) is similar to the two previous species. The cap is hemispherical at first, but becomes convex or almost flat, and has a diameter of 7–15 centimetres. It is a fine reddish-brown or bay colour, and slightly velvety. The pores are angular, ochre-yellow in the adult mushroom, and turn greenish when touched. The stalk is tapered at both ends and ochre-yellow with large brown patches. The yellowish-white flesh becomes bluish-green when cut. It is edible, and grows in broadleaf (mainly chestnut) and coniferous woods.

One large *Boletus* which grows in both broadleaf and coniferous woods deserves an individual mention. This is *Boletus calopus* (= *Boletus olivaceus*), whose cap,

measuring 10–16 centimetres in diameter, is olive-brown. The pores are yellowish too, turning to olive, and show blue patches when touched. The stalk is slightly ventricose— that is, bellied out—yellowish, and lighter-coloured at the top where it has a reticulum. At a point on the stalk, towards the lower part, its colour changes to red, especially in young specimens, with a light-coloured reticulum. The flesh is off-white and turns blue when it is exposed to the air. It emits an unpleasant smell and is bitter. There is some dispute as to whether or not this species is poisonous, but the flesh gives off an unpleasant smell and is in any event bitter in taste, and therefore inedible.

Another Bolete that is considered by some to be a variety of *Boletus calopus* is *Boletus albidus*. It has a whitish cap and a yellow stalk, without the red colour which identifies the two preceding species, and with a white reticulum.

The red-pored Boletes, a major group of *Boletus* species, although not all poisonous, should not be eaten. *Boletus satanas*, the only truly poisonous species, is most commonly to be found in beech woods on calcareous soil. *Boletus luridus*, the similar *Boletus miniatoporus*, *Boletus queletii* and *Boletus purpureus* belong to the group which changes colour. Their flesh, which ranges from whitish to pale-yellow, turns blue-green when cut.

Boletus luridus has a cap which is initially olive-brown and later turns darker. It is 6–15 centimetres in diameter, and is subtly velvety; the pores are red and the tubules initially yellow, and then greenish. The stalk, which is sometimes large but more usually slender, is yellow at the top and red-brown or earth-coloured at the bottom. It has a conspicuous purple-brown reticulum with elongated webs. It is highly esteemed as an edible variety, but must be well cooked. It grows in both broadleaf (especially chestnut) and coniferous woods.

A very similar species is *Boletus miniatoporus* or *Boletus erythropus* (Fries), which has a browner cap and does not have a reticulum on the stalk, but, in the upper part, fine, close red dots. It is highly esteemed, like *Boletus luridus*, as an edible species.

Another 'red' Bolete is Quelet's Boletus (Persoon's *Boletus erythropus* = *Boletus*

Above: Boletus chrysenteron is a common fungus of woodland. The flesh is reddish underneath the cracked skin

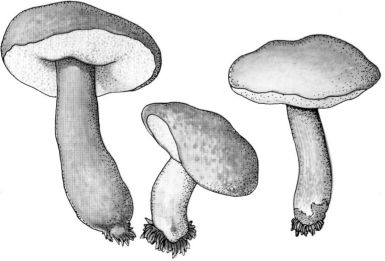

Left: Two specimens of Boletus castaneus and one of Boletus subtomentosus (right). The latter species often has a cracked cap, with yellowish flesh

Above: Boletus luridus has striking orange-red pores, and flesh that, like that of several other species, turns blue on bruising
Right: Boletus badius is an edible species

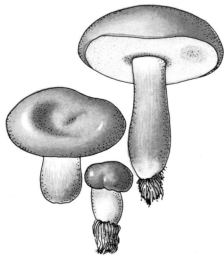

queletii), which differs from the above species by having pores which remain yellow for a longer period and quite purple flesh at the base of the stalk.

The rare *Boletus purpureus* is a handsome fungus which might well be described as decorative. Many consider it synonymous with *Boletus rhodoxanthus.* It is sturdy and grows to a considerable size. Its cap may reach 15 centimetres in diameter, and is very thick, with a variety of possible colourings. It may be cream-coloured, pinkish-ochre or reddish-grey and may even occur in an almost purple-brown colour with yellowish or dark markings. The small pores are very close together and deep blood-red in colour. The stalk is usually slightly ventricose, and yellow, especially at the top, with a handsome reticulum covered with small patches the same colour as the pores. The flesh is yellow and swiftly turns blue when exposed to the air. This species does not have a pleasant smell and the taste is somewhat bitter. It is not edible, even though some people consider that it can be eaten after lengthy preparation.

The Russulas

Another group of fungi commonly found in broadleaf woods is the Russulas. One species which may be found in oak woods is the tasty green Agaric *Russula virescens*. It has an hemispherical cap which becomes unevenly flat or slightly depressed in mature specimens. It is usually humped or wavy,

white at first and then speckled with light-green or olive markings. This fungus cracks open to reveal white, unchanging flesh with a sweetish smell. The gills are white and sometimes forked while the stalk is squat, cylindrical, white, and spongy inside.

The second species worthy of mention is *Russula cyanoxantha*, of which there are two forms, one with a dark-green cap, the other with a violet-wine-coloured (fairly dark) cap. The two colours are often pale and merge almost indistinguishably. In both cases the slightly slimy cap, 6—15 centimetres in diameter, is not very thick and has fine radial streaks. The gills are white, greasy and often forked (bifurcate). The stalk, which is not squat, is solid and white.

The flesh is also white, unchanging, and has no smell, but it has a pleasant nutty taste. It is excellent to eat, and grows in autumn in broadleaf woodland, particularly chestnut and beech woods. *Russula grisea*, another edible species, also has a green cap, but the gills tend to be straw-coloured.

The following Russulas are among those whose caps range in colour from violet to crimson. *Russula olivacea* has a red, brownish-red or olive-brown cap, gills which eventually turn yellow and a white stalk with pink patches. *Russula sardonia* has a wine-coloured cap which is conspicuously jagged around the edge, with creamy gills, and often occurs with lilac-coloured shades at the edge and a stalk which is the same

Top: Russula virescens is an edible species, with a verdigris green cap
Above: Russula cyanoxantha is an edible species which likes beech woods
Above left: Boletus miniatoporus or erythropus is an edible species to be found on poor soil in woods generally

57

Right: The aptly named Sickener is seen in various stages of development

colour as the cap. Its flesh has a burning taste. The rare *Russula azurea,* whose cap ranges in colour from lilac to pale blue, has white gills and a white stalk which is slightly swollen at the base. *Russula violacea,* an occasional species of chestnut woods, has a violet wine-coloured cap and straw-coloured gills. Finally *Russula atropurpurea,* found mainly in oak woods, has a purple cap and rust-spotted gills, and also has flesh which is very hot to the taste.

There are numerous red-capped Russulas of different shades, and it is often quite a problem to identify them precisely because of this variety of colour. Sometimes these shades are quite pale if the cap has been washed by prolonged rain. There are various chemical tests which can be used to distinguish the species, but this is clearly beyond the capacities of the casual visitor to the woods, and, as will be seen, some care must be exercised in the gathering of these confusing species.

One of the commonest of these is the Sickener (*Russula emetica*), found invariably in coniferous woods. It is relatively small, (6–9 centimetres) with the cap initially spherical, and then, as the fungus grows, hemispherical, and finally flat or depressed at the centre. It is invariably scarlet in colour, and striate at the edge in adult specimens. The gills are white, as is the stalk, which is cylindrical, club-shaped or slightly irregular, and usually longer than the cap is wide. The flesh is white (pinkish beneath the skin of the cap) and very acrid. It is a poisonous species, but becomes harmless when cooked. The beech wood form of this species is *Russula mairei,* slightly smaller than *Russula emetica,* with completely white flesh and a stipe no longer than the cap diameter.

Two more Russulas which may be confused, but which to help identification, can be said generally to occur in different woodland habitats, are *Russula lepida* and *Russula sanguinea.* Both have red caps and reddish stalks, but the former has a straight stalk and occurs in deciduous woods, while the latter has a tapering stalk and is found under conifers. Both have white gills. Another species, *Russula rosea,* is very similar to *Russula lepida* in form, but is confined to beech woods and has a white stalk.

The group of red-capped Russulas also includes Romell's Russula (*Russula romellii*) and *Russula aurata.* The first may occasionally be reddish, but is more usually purplish, with a striate edge to the cap. The gills range from white to yellowish, but the stalk and edible flesh are white. *Russula aurata* has a cap which may reach ten centimetres in

Left: Russulas are often difficult to identify. Russula olivacea is an edible species rather similar to several others
Below: Lactarius scrobiculatus is one of the acrid, inedible Milk Caps

diameter, is slightly slimy (or viscous), and orange-red to yellow in colour. The gills are white, passing to yellowish with a white edge. The stalk is whitish or light yellow and the flesh is white, very delicate, sweet and slightly acrid. This is an edible species which grows in summer in shady woods.

The Milk Caps
Close relatives of the Russulas are the Milk Caps, so-called because they ooze a kind of latex (white or coloured depending on the species) if broken. As fully grown specimens, the Milk Caps generally have a funnel-shaped cap but this is initially more or less convex with curled edges.

One of the commonest and largest species of broadleaf woodlands is the Peppery Milk Cap (*Lactarius piperatus*), found in many kinds of deciduous woods in the late summer. Its cap, which develops rapidly until it has become depressed, may reach a diameter of 15 centimetres and is milk-white turning to slightly ochreous in fully grown specimens. The gills are close together, white or slightly yellowish and decurrent. The stalk, also white, is squat and cylindrical. The flesh, which is the same colour, oozes a white milk which is very peppery on the tongue. Despite this, this mushroom is much used as a supplementary food in

eastern European countries such as Poland and Lithuania. Slices of the flesh are conserved in salt, or dried. In some regions the dried and pulverized fungus takes the place of pepper in the kitchen. However, its caustic quality is not to everybody's taste, and in certain cases, this species can also cause gastroenteric disorders.

Closely related in appearance to the Peppery Milk Cap are *Lactarius vellereus* and *Lactarius controversus*. The first has a distinctive velvety surface, with gills that are weakly decurrent, and a cap that becomes centrally depressed when mature. The second species can be easily identified from these other Milk Caps by its gills, which are pale pink in colour.

Another species which is fairly like the two preceding ones is the very rare *Lactarius scrobiculatus*. The cap, which may reach a diameter of 20 centimetres, is ochre-yellow, and usually slightly concentrically zoned (with alternate dark and light bands). The gills are cream-coloured and decurrent while the stalk is the same colour as the cap and has numerous distinctive pits (foveae). The flesh and milk are whitish and turn yellow as the fungus ages. It is an acrid, inedible fungus which is found from summer to autumn in both broadleaf and coniferous woods.

Among the other Milk Caps is another noteworthy species, *Lactarius torminosus* — so-called because it has violently purgative properties if swallowed. It has apparently also been the cause of serious cases of poisoning. The cap, which varies from 4—8 centimetres in diameter, is convex at first, and then concave, conspicuously inward-curled at the edge and downy. The colour of the cap is a fleshy pink contoured with lighter concentric zones. The stalk is whitish with reddish shades, and is also slightly velvety in some cases. This is a fungus of mixed woods and heaths, with white and somewhat acid flesh, and a milk that has rather an acrid taste. *Lactarius pubescens* is very similar, although it is lighter in colour. This species, however, is more particularly allied with birch trees.

Certain other Milk Caps, less important in this genera, are peculiar to sunny deciduous woods: *Lactarius uvidus*, *Lactarius subdulcis*, *Lactarius quietus* and *Lactarius turpis*. *Lactarius uvidus* has a cap which eventually becomes concave and slightly viscous. The cap ranges in colour from the usual grey to olive or bistre, tinged with lilac. The gills are whitish initially, becoming progressively more ochreous. The stalk is also whitish or pale grey. It is an occasional species found in deciduous woods, especially under birches, from summer to autumn. It should be considered among the suspect species, although its flesh is tasteless. Bruised flesh turns lilac, but the milk is unchanging.

Lactarius subdulcis is a mild but slightly bitter-tasting Milk Cap which is edible but poor. This species also grows in deciduous woods, particularly with beech. Its cap is initially flat-convex and slightly rounded, then funnel-shaped, and fairly tan-coloured. The slightly decurrent gills are cream-coloured at first, and eventually become reddish. The stalk is slightly paler than the cap and tapers at the base.

Lactarius quietus is very like the previous species, but its milk is without the bitter tang of the *subdulcis* Milk Cap. It is also edible but poor, and common during the autumn in oak woods. The leather or cinnamon coloured cap is concentrically zoned. The gills are lighter than the cap, as is the stalk, especially at the top. Its milk is white-yellow and mild.

Lactarius turpis is slightly larger than *Lactarius quietus*, with a cap that may reach a diameter of 14 centimetres. Convex initially, the cap becomes flatter, and finally becomes depressed. Its colour is dark olive-brown, and paler at the edge, while the gills are whitish or straw-coloured and turn brown when touched. The stalk is somewhat squat, smooth or pitted, and lighter than the cap. It grows most often near birch trees in early autumn. Although considered poisonous or at least suspect, it is strictly speaking harmless, but its consumption is not to be recommended.

The Tricholoma fungi
Following the Milk Caps, another large and common group of fungi found in deciduous woods is the genus *Tricholoma*. Three of the commonest species are: *Tricholoma saponaceum*, *Tricholoma fulvum* and *Tricholoma sulphureum*.

The first, *Tricholoma saponaceum*, forms rings or lines in summer and autumn and has a cap 3—8 centimetres in diameter. It is fleshy and convex in young specimens, but becomes progressively flatter, sometimes with an umbo. The caps of this species are usually somewhat irregular and wavy. The colour varies from bistre to blackish- and olive-grey, but is always slightly darker at the centre.

The gills are quite wide apart, whitish with greenish highlights and, in adult specimens, reddish markings. The stalk is cylindrical or ventricose and spindle-shaped (fusiform). It is quite slender, often roots like an ordinary plant, and is whitish in colour. Although this species is not harmful, it is poor to eat.

Tricholoma fulvum is a mushroom of average size, identifiable by its fleshy, flattish, reddish cap. The gills are yellow and the stalk yellowish at the top becoming gradually brown towards the tapering base. The whitish flesh smells of flour and is slightly bitter; as a result, although not poisonous, it is not worth eating. The flesh of the stalk is a definite yellow colour. This species grows in peaty soil in mixed woodland, especially in association with birches.

Tricholoma sulphureum, as the name suggests, is completely sulphur-yellow, but sometimes the centre of the cap is brownish in colour. The gills are widely separated (distant) and the stalk is relatively slender and sometimes slightly striate. The flesh is also yellow, and emits a noxious smell rather like coal gas, which makes it a fungus to avoid. It is a species of deciduous woodland generally, but especially of oak wood.

A fungus which is sometimes found in oak woods, and especially in clayey-calcareous soil, is *Hygrophorus russula* (= *Tricholoma russula*). It has a fleshy, convex, then flat and finally depressed cap, 8–20 centimetres in diameter. The cap has a slightly viscous texture, with a distinctive fleshy or purple colour, and is fairly speckled. The gills of this edible species are white with red patches.

The last of these species, *Tricholoma nudum* (= *Lepista nuda*), commonly known as the Wood Blewits, is almost uniformly a beautiful violet colour. The cap is convex at first and then fairly flattened, with reddish-brown shades at the centre on a light violet background. The gills are close together and the stalk is fibrillous, that is, covered with fibrous strands, and slightly swollen at the base where there is usually a whitish mycelium. The flesh is also light violet, faintly scented and somewhat acid. This species is good to eat, and is common during the autumn and winter when it may be found in deciduous and coniferous woods where there is plenty of humus.

Cortinarius species

The genus *Cortinarius* includes fungi which are so called because they have a distinctive curtain—a fairly thin, silky, cobweb-like veil (cortina). This veil or curtain joins the edge of the cap to the stalk in the young stage. Among the commonest species in mixed woods is *Cortinarius* (= *Inoloma*) *albo-violaceus*. This species has a violet-white cap and lilac-coloured gills which turn reddish-brown because of the colour of the spores. The stalk is slightly bulbous at the base, slightly thinner at the top and the same colour as the cap. The veil is white and silky at first, then turns rust-coloured because of the spores which fall into its filaments. The flesh is pale lilac or almost white and edible. This fungus grows in oak and beech woods.

Other violet-coloured members of this group include *Cortinarius violaceus* which, in colour, calls to mind the beautiful violet

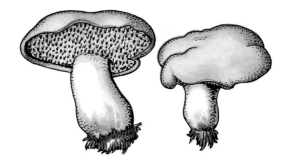

Top to bottom:
Lactarius turpis,
Tricholoma fulvum,
Cortinarius praestans
and Hydnum repandum

of *Tricholoma nudum,* although it is an even more intense violet. The cap changes from its initial hemispherical shape to a convex or almost flat form. The gills are the same colour as the cap initially but change to a rust colour as the spores mature. The stalk, which is quite slender, is also violet and fibrillous. The violet-grey flesh is not very tasty, but is edible. This is a very rare species in Great Britain although it is occasionally found in Scotland.

The large and tasty *Cortinarius praestans* somewhat resembles the Cep at first glance. Of course, there is a primary distinction in that *Cortinarius praestans* has gills instead of pores and tubules. Its cap, which develops from a hemispherical to a convex shape as the fungus matures, is reddish-brown in colour. Often the cap is found with shades of violet and white over much of its area, but this is generally a feature of the initial stages of growth. The gills are quite close together, white at first, then lilac-coloured with straw-coloured tints, and eventually ochreous. The stalk, which is rather squat, solid, bulbous at the base and slightly thinner at the top, is white with violet patches, and fibrillous. The flesh, which is also white and tinted with lilac, is scented and has a pleasant taste. This fungus, which appears between the summer and the autumn, is occasionally found in a variety of deciduous woods.

Tree stump growths

A distinctive gilled fungus is the Spindle Shank (*Collybia fusipes*). Very common in summer and autumn, this species grows in clusters, which are often very large, on oak and beech stumps. The cap is not very fleshy, and develops from a convex into a flat shape. It is sometimes wavy, and reddish-brown or greyish-brown in colour. The gills, which are set very far apart and joined by veins, are ivory-white and develop reddish patches if touched. The stalk is spindle-shaped, grooved and reddish-brown, but becomes dark-coloured or almost black at the base. Although the cap is considered to be edible when young—the stalk should not be eaten at any stage of its growth—this species is best ignored; it has an elastic texture and can cause gastroenteric disorders.

A very rare fungus found on stumps is *Pleurotus olearius* (= *Clitocybe olearia*). It is fairly large, growing as tall as 15 centimetres and sometimes more. The cap is orange-brown and finely striate, in shape convex at first, but becoming conspicuously funnel-shaped, and often quite irregular. The thin, close and decurrent gills are a fine, bright orange-yellow in colour. The stalk is tall, tapering at the base and slightly wavy. This is a poisonous fungus and has the distinctive feature of being slightly luminous at night. There are several fungus species which have this property, which is the result of photosynthesis in reverse. Food is consumed by the fungus to produce light, rather than light being absorbed to produce energy for food production.

Deciduous woods, in particular oak and chestnut, are host to another of the Polypores, the unusual *Grifola frondosa.* This species, which is often found in very large tufts, has a repeatedly and irregularly ramified or branched stalk, and small, oyster-shaped, often lobate, brown caps. The flesh is firm and very white and is edible when this species is very young.

Woodland curiosities

Late summer and autumn is the time to find the large bracket-shaped forms of the Beefsteak Fungus (*Fistulina hepatica*). This species is dark red and viscous on the upper surface, and white flecked with reddish-brown below. Like *Grifola frondosa,* it is only edible when young and after boiling. It is found particularly on oaks, occuring on the trunks of the living trees, and is responsible for a disease called 'Brown Oak'.

Other unusual fungi found in deciduous woodlands include the Tooth Fungi, of which *Hydnum repandum* is the commonest. It is a capped species, slightly squat and irregular, with an ochre-white stalk. The cap is slightly humped on the upper surface, and a buff colour. Underneath the cap, there are neither gills nor pores, but delicate spines which are white or the same colour as the cap. Its closest relative, *Hydnum rufescens,* has a more orange-coloured cap. Both are edible but somewhat hard to digest because of the tough texture of the flesh and the bitter taste, which can, however, be removed by boiling. The former is a species of deciduous woodland, while the latter also occurs among conifers.

Another unusual species is the Horn of Plenty (*Craterellus cornucopioides*), a fungus which has the shape of a small trumpet. It is hollow inside, 4–8 centimetres high, with thin, elastic flesh. The upper surface is scaly and wavy at the edge, dark-grey or blackish-brown in colour and its lower surface is smooth or slightly wrinkled. It is good to eat, though the flesh is tough, and this species may also be successfully dried. The Horn of Plenty is a fairly common species found in summer and autumn among the dead leaves of deciduous woods.

The Truffles comprise another interesting group found in deciduous woods. These are subterranean, or hypogeal, fungi, celebrated for the distinctive, penetrating, aromatic smell which makes them of such commercial value. The two mostly highly prized species are the white Piedmont Truffle (*Tuber magnatum*) and the black Perigord Truffle (*Tuber melanosporum*), neither of which is found in the British Isles.

The first is the size of a walnut, but may reach the size of an ordinary potato. It is irregular and slightly gnarled, while the Perigord Truffle is slightly smaller, more regular, and covered with rough polygonal warts. The flesh of both species consists of a compact mass of hyphae which form tiny cavities containing the asci. Overall they have a rather contorted appearance, which belies their exquisite taste. In Britain, only *Tuber rufum*, *Tuber nitidum* and *Tuber aestivum* occur, the latter two being rare. *Tuber rufum* is a reddish, rounded Truffle which is quite small and is found in deciduous woods on rich soil. *Tuber nitidum* is similarly small and found in rich soil. *Tuber aestivum*, however, grows up to nine centimetres in diameter and in appearance is close to *Tuber melanosporum*. At one time this Truffle was collected on a large scale from the beech woods of Southern England.

Birch wood fungi

The birch trees (*Betula* species) and their hybrids, which occur on acidic soil or in exposed, upland situations, also have a wide variety of associated fungus species. In lowland habitats, birches are short-lived, fast-growing trees which normally represent a transitional stage in the development of woodland, either taking over in the early stages of oak wood regeneration or in the

Above: Lactarius torminosus is an inedible Milk Cap Right: The Horn of Plenty is an excellent species which is easily dried

Right: This section of a white Truffle shows the white flesh and the darker, spore-forming gleba. All the Truffles have a similar structure

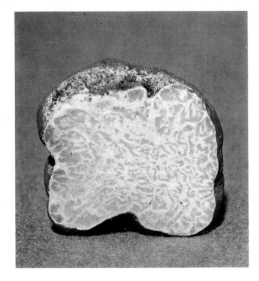

development of pine woods on sandy soils. Their wood is soft and decays rapidly after being attacked by any of a number of fungi. It is a common sight in some areas to see dead or dying trees supporting a number of fruiting bodies of the Birch Polypore (*Piptoporus betulinus*). Their sessile structures are shell-shaped and rounded, brownish above and white below. This species is a harmful parasite. It causes damage which eventually kills the tree, and then feeds off the dead wood. This ability to feed off both living and dead material is termed facultative.

Two species of *Trametes,* another Polypore genus, are also found on birch wood. *Trametes cinnabarina* is a reddish-orange bracket fungus occurring mainly on birch, but also found on beech. The brackets are up to nine centimetres in diameter, very corky and thick, with blood-red pores. *Trametes betulina* (= *Lenzites betulina*) is up to eight centimetres across, with a woolly, white-grey surface which is zoned brown. Neither of these species is particularly common.

Another species occasionally found growing on birch is *Pholiota (Flammula) apicrea.* This is a gilled fungus with a long stalk and a small convex to flattened cap which is yellow or olive in colour.

Among the fungi found growing under birches are many species of *Cortinarius.* One of the two commonest is *Cortinarius pholideus,* which has a convex, brown and scaly cap and a slender stalk also covered in dark scales. The other, *Cortinarius semisanguineus,* has a slender, flexuose (curved) stalk and an olive cap with an umbo and an overall diameter of five centimetres. The gills turn rusty as they mature. Other *Cortinarius* species include *Cortinarius armillatus,* a large, striking fungus with a convex, red-brown cap and a lighter stalk which has reddish belts in the lower part. *Cortinarius flexipes* is very small and has a characteristic Geranium smell. The stalk is cottony and the umbonate cap is dark brown. *Cortinarius delibutus* has a golden yellow cap which is smooth and viscid, and a stalk which is yellow tinged with blue at the top, above a ring zone.

Among the Amanitas found in birch woods, one of the commonest is the Fly Agaric (*Amanita muscaria*), together with the Tawny Grisette (*Amanita fulva*). Various

Boletes are also commonly associated with birch. The most unusual is *Boletus parasiticus,* which is a small fungus found as a parasite on Earth-balls (*Scleroderma* sp.). *Boletus testaceoscaber* is, by contrast, a large species with a yellowish or reddish-orange cap and a striate stalk which is dark and covered in scales. *Boletus scaber* has a tall stalk covered similarly with scurfy scales, and a greyish-brown cap which is smooth when mature.

Two Russulas are found by birches. One is *Russula claroflava,* a bright yellow species with a white stalk that becomes greyish when mature. *Russula nitida* is wine-red in colour, having a furrowed margin and cream gills. The stalk is flushed with pink or red and is hollow in mature specimens.

Beech wood fungi

Beech woods are one of the most aesthetically pleasing forms of woodland, being graceful, cool and inviting. The beech is widely distributed both in mixed woodlands on light soil and also as a dominant species on chalk. The reason for its appearance on these types of contrasting soil—one acid and the other alkaline—seems to be the common factor of good drainage.

In the latter habitat, the beech trees usually form pure woods, or 'stands' as they are called. Because of the way in which the beech grows and the leaves overlap to form a continuous canopy, the light level in a beech wood is usually low. This, together with the inherent good drainage of the soil and the effectiveness of the beech itself in drawing out all the water, leads to little else being able to grow.

The flora of such a wood tends to be fairly distinctive, whether the soil is acid or alkaline. While there are few flowering plants which will tolerate these conditions, the fungal flora tends to be relatively rich. Some of these fungi are also found in other types of wood, but many of them are restricted to beech. This is true of fungal flora all over Europe, and in western regions of Asia, both high up and in the lowlands.

Right: Beech wood in spring. Note the absence of groundcover vegetation
Far right, top: Boletus appendiculatus
Far right, centre: Boletus satanas, occasionally found in beech woods
Far right, bottom: Lactarius scrobiculatus

There are numerous fungi found in beech woods, many of them restricted to this habitat. One of the largest groups found here is the Boletes. The best *Boletus* to be found in beech woods, *Boletus aereus,* has been mentioned above. It is distinctive for its rather thickset shape, the dark sepia-brown cap and the white, unchanging flesh.

Another Bolete found in beech woods is the uncommon *Boletus appendiculatus* which is particularly good to eat. It likes open places and grows to a considerable size—the cap may have a diameter of up to 20 centimetres. In general appearance, it resembles the Cep, but the stalk tends to taper towards the base and the cap is opaque, reddish-brown or ochre-coloured above and pinkish-brown beneath the skin of the cap. The pores are sulphur-yellow, tending to turn blue if touched, and the fine reticulum at the top of the stalk is the same colour. The stalk is brown towards the base. The flesh itself is firm and yellow and, though it sometimes scarcely alters at all when exposed to the air, it often becomes slightly greenish-blue when cut. *Boletus regius* is sturdier in appearance than *Boletus appendiculatus,* the cap being pinkish-red and tending to be wine-coloured or brick-coloured. Whatever the variation, the cap is brightly coloured, and the stalk is yellower than that of *Boletus appendiculatus.* Neither of these species is confined exclusively to beech woods.

Very akin to *Boletus appendiculatus* is *Boletus impolitus,* which also has a slightly rooting stem and the same colouring and tones. However, it lacks a conspicuous reticulum at the top of the stalk, although it does have tiny, scaly, yellow flakes. This species is uncommon and, as well as being found in beech woods, grows in other broadleaf woods, especially on calcareous ground.

In beech wood on acid soils, one may also come across at least three other species: *Boletus radicans, Boletus* (= *Xerocomus*) *subtomentosus* and *Boletus* (= *Xerocomus*) *chrysenteron.* The two latter species have already been described earlier but the broadleaf wood is also host to *Boletus radicans* (= *Boletus albidus*). This has a stem that tapers towards the base, and is rooting. The general colouring ranges through the yellows, except for the cap which is greyish or brown-grey. The flesh is yellow and bitter, and as such the mushroom is not worth eating.

There is yet another Bolete found among beeches, but this species likes beech woods where the soil is calcareous. This is *Boletus satanas,* which, although it is the only poisonous Boletus, is not deadly. This fungus may reach a fair size and is squat in shape. The initially hemispherical cap turns convex and ends up almost flat. Above, it is light ochre-grey or almost whitish, with shades of pale olive-green. The pores beneath the cap are very small, yellowish to start with, progressing through bright blood-red to a final stage, in very developed specimens, of orange and ochre-yellow. The stalk is swollen in the lower half and yellow in the upper part where it has a distinctive bright red fine reticulum. Lower down it passes to a reddish and then ochre-grey colour. The flesh is whitish but, as soon as it is cut, turns reddish and then swiftly to blue, emitting an unpleasant smell. Similarly, the pores turn greenish and bluish if touched.

There are several Russulas found mainly associated with beech. Apart from *Russula cyanoxantha,* which has already been described, *Russula fellea* is also peculiar to beech woods. It has a foul, extremely bitter and acrid taste, although the flesh itself smells of Geraniums. It is of average size and has a straw-coloured to ochre cap which is depressed and striate at the edge. The gills are whitish and, in the adult fungus, assume the same colour as the cap. The stalk is similarly coloured or perhaps a little paler, and slightly hollow.

Russula mairei and *Russula olivacea* are both confined to beech woods. The inedible *mairei* species is a smaller version of the Sickener (*Russula emetica*) having a scarlet cap, white flesh, gills and stalk and giving off a faint smell of honey. The latter species is also red, but with brown or olive tints, yellow gills and a white pink-suffused stalk. The cap, which is 8–15 centimetres in diameter, is concentrically colour-zoned with a pale edge. This is an edible species in contrast with the Sickener and its close relatives.

Another Russula, *Russula rosea,* can be easily confused with *Russula mairei* since it is also confined to beech woods and has a white stalk. The colour of its cap is rose-red,

Right: Ramaria botrytis is an edible species of broadleaf woods with acid humus

however, and the white flesh is spongy, without any taste or smell.

The green *Russula virescens* has already been mentioned as being relatively common in broadleaf woods, but it is also one of the typical fungi found in beech woods. It is a very distinctive fungus with a cracked, green and granular cap. The tapering stalk, the flesh and gills are all white or slightly cream-coloured. This, too, is an edible species.

Apart from the various Milk Caps found generally in broadleaf woods—species such as *Lactarius volemus, Lactarius scrobiculatus* and *Lactarius piperatus*—there are several species which are particularly found in beech woods. These include *Lactarius pallidus, Lactarius blennius* and *Lactarius subdulcis.*

The first species, which is inedible, is restricted to beech woods, and has a moderately large cap, 6–12 centimetres in diameter. The colour is tan, sometimes pinkish and the milk is bitter and white. The cap is eventually depressed in the centre, concealing the crowded gills.

Lactarius blennius is also inedible, with an acrid milk that turns grey on exposure. The cap is similarly depressed in the centre, but it is brown and green in colour and is covered with dark spots. The stout stalk is the same colour as the cap. Both species appear during the summer and autumn.

Lactarius subdulcis is a small, tan-coloured species with a depressed cap, and paler, decurrent gills. The milk is an unchanging white and usually slightly bitter in taste.

Lactarius fulvissimus is a Milk Cap found on chalky soils, and hence quite commonly among beech trees. This has an orange cap and stalk, with paler, slightly decurrent gills.

The Amanitas which are found in beech woods include *Amanita citrina* (= *Amanita mappa*), *Amanita junquillea* (= *Amanita gemmata*) and *Amanita excelsa*. All of these species have already been discussed and the first two are easily identifiable, *Amanita citrina* by its pale lemon-yellow cap and *Amanita junquillea* by its bright yellow cap with whitish scales or large warts. In both species the gills, ring and stalk are all white.

Amanita excelsa is a medium-sized edible fungus which is not quite so distinctive. Its cap, which becomes rapidly flattened, is an ash greyish-brown and has large, thinly

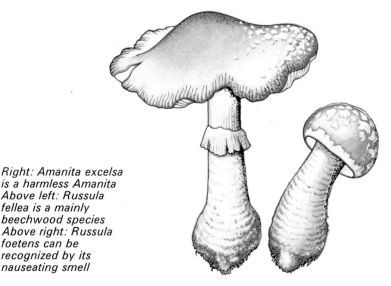

Right: Amanita excelsa is a harmless Amanita
Above left: Russula fellea is a mainly beechwood species
Above right: Russula foetens can be recognized by its nauseating smell

Above: Clavaria
pistillaris is one of the
fairy clubs found in
broadleaf woods
Above right: Two
examples of Ramaria
botrytis

distributed warts. The gills and stalk are white and these characteristics together with the conspicuously striate stalk above the ring, are probably the best way of identifying it.

Of the various types of *Tricholoma* found in beech woods, a frequent one is *Tricholoma argyraceum*. Also found in other broadleaf and coniferous woods, it prefers beech woods on chalk. It is edible, and of average size. The cap, hemispherical at first, is almost flat in mature specimens, and is slightly irregular round the edge and often umbonate. Its colour varies from grey to light bistre or brown and has numerous small scales which are darker in colour and especially dense towards the centre. The gills are white or greyish, yellowing later and the stalk is cylindrical, hollow, and grey or white in colour. No ring is present and the flesh is also white, unchanging and has a mealy taste.

Among the species of *Cortinarius* which are found here is *Cortinarius melleolens*, a species which is locally common. It is of average size with a fleshy cap, convex at first, then almost flat, being pale ochre in colour, darker at the centre. The silky surface is often covered with the remnants of the veil that protected the gills. The stalk is tall and slender, bulbous at the base and white or faintly yellow. The veil is white and short-lived. The flesh is white, yellowish in the stalk and light brown in the bulbous base, turning generally ochre with age.

A second species found almost exclusively in beech woods is *Cortinarius calochrous* with a yellow cap, lilac-purple gills and a yellowish-white stalk. The flesh is the same colour as the latter, and is edible. *Cortinarius elatior* is also found mainly among beech trees. It is distinctive for its stalk, which is rooting and scaly. The cap and gills are both brown at maturity.

Among the gilled fungi it is quite common to find species of the genus *Inocybe* in beech woods. There are over 80 species in this genus, most of them poisonous, and almost all inedible. They are often difficult to identify and may be confused with perfectly edible species. One of the most deadly, found in beech woods on chalk, is *Inocybe patouillardii*. This medium-size species is whitish when young, changing later to yellowish-brown. The margin of the cap is frequently cracked when mature and the flesh becomes pinkish if bruised. Like most species of *Inocybe*, this species has a definitely umbonate cap. Other species are found in beech woods, but not exclusively confined to them.

Of the fungi found growing on beech trees, the most typical and striking is *Oudemansiella mucida*. This occurs on dead trunks and weakened trees some distance from the ground, and has a distinct stalk and cap. The cap is at first very convex, becoming flatter with maturity, and is greyish or white in colour, with a shiny and slimy appearance. The gills are distant and white, while the stalk is slender and has a membranous ring. A related species, *Oude-mansiella radicata*, is not restricted to beech woods, and is a soil-dwelling fungus with a distinct 'tap root'.

Another fungus found in beech woods is *Ganoderma applanatum*, a bracket fungus up to 30 centimetres in diameter. The upper surface is humped and red-brown, while the pores are white. The flesh is brown and corky. This species causes serious heart rot in trees, particularly in beech, and can be found throughout the year. *Ganoderma lucidum* also occurs on beech, but is also common on other broadleaf trees. Unlike the previous species it has a short stalk and is dark brown in colour. The cap is concentrically grooved, and shiny, hence the specific name *lucidum*.

Occasionally various examples of the Club Fungi (*Clavaria* and *Ramaria* species) may be found in beech woods. Among those worth mentioning are *Clavaria pistillaris*, *Clavaria fistulosa* and *Ramaria botrytis*, all of which are edible species. The first two are shaped like clubs, the latter of the two being much more slender. *Ramaria botrytis* is densely branched with reddish tips and is found in the acid soil of broadleaf woods.

Fungi of Coniferous Woods

About 30 per cent of all the world's forest areas are coniferous, this type of woodland being typical of the cooler, drier Northern Hemisphere. North America, for instance, has wide areas of both natural and cultivated coniferous forest. Spruce and fir predominate in its northern latitudes, but a wider variety of coniferous types appear further south in the continent. Despite its commonness in temperate regions, woodland formed by coniferous species varies tremendously in its richness as a habitat, as is demonstrated by three different types of conifer—Yew, Juniper and Scots Pine.

The Yew may form quite dense stands on chalk soil where woodland is regenerating, but it is a species normally found wild in mixed woodland on either chalky or acid soils. Very few fungi are ever found in woodland where Yew is well established.

The Scots Pine is widely distributed, being particularly common on acid and highland soils, and frequently occurring in mixed woodland. It is commonly found with birches in certain areas, particularly on heathlands where it thrives. In the British Isles it is native to upland Scotland, where it exists as a particular form, *Pinus sylvatica* var. *scotica*. Elsewhere, it has become common as a result of widespread planting and in places where woods have been cleared on light, sandy soil.

Coniferous trees, of course, are the basis of forestry in most temperate countries. Most

Above: A natural pinewood with its dense groundcover of acid-loving flora

Right: Boletus granulatus is a typical Bolete of coniferous woods
Below: Boletus luteus is a coniferous species often found in grass
Bottom: Telltale cones and needles reveal that Boletus bovinus is found under pines

conifers found in Britain, for example, are introduced and planted by Man for timber. This situation contrasts somewhat with that in Continental Europe and North America. There various conifer species form vast tracts of natural woodland, although coniferous forestry plantations are also widespread. In Britain, the Scots Pine is associated in Southern woodlands with the Whortleberry (*Vaccinium myrtillus*), various heathers and bracken, some grasses such as *Deschampsia flexuosa* and *Molinia caerulea.* Very little else will grow in this kind of woodland, apart from mosses such as *Leucobryum glaucum* and *Sphagnum,* and some liverworts. Scottish pine woods include a much wider range of species. Many of these, such as Lesser Twayblade, Wintergreens, Coralroot Orchid and *Linnaea borealis,* are rare.

Among other pine species, are two of the forms of *Pinus nigra* — the Austrian Pine (var. *nigra*) and the Corsican Pine (var. *laricio*). The former is recognized by its rather rigid, straight leaves and the latter by its twisted leaves. Both have green leaves which are more than ten centimetres long and which, like the other 90 *Pinus* species, are borne in groups on short side-shoots. In Britain, spruces (*Picea* species) and firs (*Abies* species) are also widely planted. The spruces have pendulous cones, whorled leaves and permanent woody pegs at the bases of the leaves. The Norway Spruce (*Picea abies*) is distinguished from the Sitka Spruce (*Picea sitchensis*) in having four-sided leaves rather than flat ones. The Western Hemlock (*Tsuga heterophylla*) is similar to the spruces, but has stalked leaves and small cones.

The firs, however, have upright cones and leaves arranged in two rows. They are less planted for forestry than the spruces, but there are several species which have been used. The Douglas Fir (*Pseudotsuga menziesii*) is similar to the firs, but has pendulous cones. Of the cypresses, only Western Red Cedar (*Thuja plicata*) is planted on any scale, although various cypresses are planted as ornamentals or for hedging.

Deciduous conifers used for forestry include the European Larch (*Larix decidua*), with yellowish twigs and upright cone scales; and the Japanese Larch (*Larix leptolepis*), with reddish twigs and reflexed cone scales.

Most forestry woodland is close planted and well managed. The result is a highly groomed habitat with little dead or decaying material and low light levels which prevent most other plants from growing. Most broadleaf woods are composed of deciduous trees and are, in general, lighter, more fertile places because their leaves usually decay readily to give rich, non-acid humus. Coniferous needles, by contrast, decay only slowly, giving an acid humus low in nutrients. This basic difference in fertility affects all the other species sharing the habitat. A comparison between a pine wood and an oak wood will immediately show how the former has virtually no flowering plants growing there, while the latter has a rich variety of species. This contrast is not completely reflected in the fungi which are found in the two types of woodland, but are nevertheless fairly distinctive, because the environments are so very different.

The range of fungi species which grow on dead or decaying wood is enormous. While some are specific to only one type of wood, there are many which can be found on a wide variety of different woods. It must be remembered, though, that most woodland fungi are soil-growing and among these fungi is to be found a certain degree of preference for a particular type of tree species. However, since a great many woodlands are mixed in their composition, the individual preferences of fungus species may become obscured by the variety of apparent opportunities.

There are very few fungi which are specifically found with only one conifer species. Most of the fungi found in conifer woods are species which are capable of attacking coniferous wood generally. Among this number are fungi which are also found in broadleaf woods. The Chantarelle (*Cantharellus cibarius*), for example, is found in both major types of wood.

The Boletes

Despite the unpromising sound of this habitat, the list of species found in conifer woods is extensive. Boletes are particularly common in coniferous woods and include *Boletus pinicola, Boletus granulatus, Boletus luteus, Boletus subtomentosus, Boletus elegans, Boletus bovinus* and *Boletus variegatus*. Many of these have been described

Above: Lactarius sanguifluus has, as its name suggests, blood-red milk
Left: Boletus luteus has yellow flesh

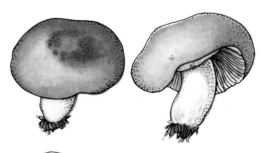

Left: Tricholomopsis rutilans is commonly found on conifer stumps
Above left: Russula vesca is an edible species often found with oaks

in the previous chapters. One species which is typical of coniferous woodland in general is *Boletus (Suillus) granulatus,* which never grows very large. Its cap, 4–10 centimetres in diameter, is hemispherical initially and develops a much flatter profile. The cap is bay-brown or ochre-coloured and invariably very slimy. The pores are sulphur-yellow and, when the fungus is young, ooze small droplets of milky liquid. The stalk is solid, cylindrical, the same colour as the pores, brown in the lower part and finely granulated at the top—hence the specific name *granulatus.* The pale yellow flesh does not change colour when cut, and emits an aromatic smell. It is a summer and autumnal species, young specimens of which are edible after being cooked. However, it is advisable to remove the slimy skin of the cap.

Boletus (Suillus) luteus is also a common species during summer and autumn in conifer woods, and likewise edible when cooked, provided that the skin of the cap is removed. Slightly larger than *Boletus granulatus,* it differs principally in the cap, which is darker on its upper surface. Furthermore, in the young stage it has a whitish or violet-tinted veil. This rises from the upper part of the stalk and protects the pores. As the fungus grows, all that remains of this veil is an irregular ring-like growth on the stalk just beneath the cap.

Boletus (= Suillus = Ixocomus) variegatus is found generally in coniferous woodland on poor soil during the summer and autumn. Of average size—6–10 centimetres in diameter—its cap is convex, eventually becoming almost flat. It may be a little slimy, ochre-coloured, with small, darker-coloured granules. The pores are olive-ochre or bistre-coloured, tending to turn bluish if touched. The cylindrical stalk is solid and slightly lighter than the cap, while the flesh is soft, yellowish, tending to turn bluish when cut, and emits a rather unpleasant smell. Because of this and the poor quality of the flesh, this Boletus is not widely eaten.

Boletus (= Suillus = Ixocomus) bovinus is also a small to average-sized fungus. The cap is hemispherical and then almost flat, slightly viscous, and ochre-coloured, usually tending to reddish, but never dark. The pores are large, angular, slightly decurrent to the stalk. Initially ochre-coloured, they tend gradually to become olive-coloured as the

fungus matures. The fairly slender stalk is glabrous and slightly paler than the cap. The flesh is rather soft, yellowish, does not change colour and is sweetish. To all intents and purposes, this mushroom, which is associated with pines, is edible, but decidedly mediocre and hard to digest.

Another Boletus which may be commonly found in conifer woods from summer to autumn is *Boletinus cavipes* (= *Boletus cavipes*). This fungus is of average size, and the cap, which is 5–12 centimetres in in diameter, is at first conical-convex and then widens out and turns flat. It is usually rounded, tawny yellow to rust-brown in colour, opaque, and completely covered with darker, downy small scales. The tubules are decurrent and the pores are large, irregular, angular or elongated, yellowish, eventually turning olive-greenish. The stalk, which is hollow from top to bottom, is cylindrical but swollen at the base, ringed and the same colour as the cap or lighter, with downy scales. The firm flesh is yellowish-white or lemon-yellow in colour. It is edible, though hard to digest, and the skin of the cap should be removed.

The major species of Bolete found in larch woods is *Boletus elegans* (= *Ixocomus elegans* = *Suillus elegans* = *Suillus grevillei*) which is small or average in size. It has a convex cap which widens out and becomes almost flat. It is 3–8 centimetres in diameter, golden yellow to tawny in colour, and sticky to the touch. The pores are small at first, then fairly large and angular, and yellow in colour. The stalk is quite slender, cylindrical or slightly swollen at the base and somewhat lighter in colour than the cap, especially at the top where there is a soft, whitish, membranous ring. This ring is all that remains of the partial veil which originally protected the tubules. These are not very conspicuous and are brownish in fully grown specimens. The flesh is yellowish, does not change colour, and has a slightly aromatic and sweetish taste. This resinous quality makes this mushroom an acquired taste which is appreciated by some and not by others. It is perfectly edible, but it is advisable first to remove the cuticle of the cap. Closely akin to it is *Boletus flavus* (= *Ixocomus flavus* = *Suillus nueschii*), slightly lighter in colour (especially on the cap which is often lemon-yellow), with pores tending to greyish, and

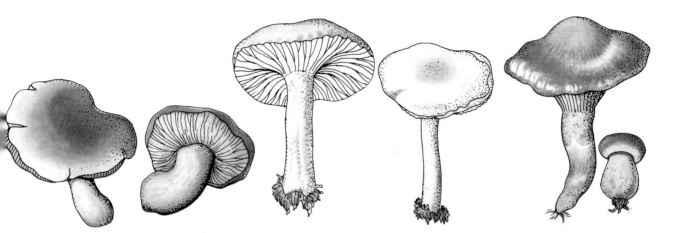

smaller in size. Some mycologists consider this fungus to be simply a variety of *Boletus elegans*.

Similar in shape and appearance are *Boletus viscidus*, and *Boletus tridentinus*, which are frequently found in larch woods. The first species, *Boletus viscidus* (= *Ixocomus viscidus* = *Suillus aeruginascens*) has, as the name suggests, a very slimy cap which is greenish-grey in colour, with a stalk, which is usually a whitish-grey.

Boletus tridentinus (= *Ixocomus tridentinus* = *Suillus tridentinus*) has a tawny to copper-coloured cap, colours which are to some extent echoed in the flesh, especially beneath the outer skin. The pores are orange-ochre, reddish or darker in more fully-grown specimens. A feature of larch woods, this species is also found under the Yew, a tree which has few fungi associated with it.

Boletus cyanescens, as its name suggests, has flesh which turns blue if cut. It is a rare fungus found especially associated with spruce. Both cap and stalk are pale ochre in colour, the stalk being cavernous, or hollow, in mature specimens.

Another species with ochre-coloured cap and stalk is *Boletus* (*Tylopilus*) *felleus*, a common species found mainly in conifer woods. The pores, however, are pink when mature and the stalk is covered with a wide-meshed network. The flesh tastes very bitter and makes the fungus unpalatable.

The Amanitas and Russulas

The genus *Amanita*, which has been thoroughly described earlier, occurs in pine woods, where *Amanita citrina*, *Amanita rubescens*, *Amanita spissa*, and *Amanita porphyria* may all be found.

The list of Russulas associated with coniferous woodland is extensive. *Russula ochroleuca*, *Russula vesca*, *Russula caerulea*, *Russula queletii*, *Russula xerampelina*, *Russula turci*, *Russula sardonia*, *Russula nauseosa*, *Russula paludosa* and *Russula puellaris* may all appear among conifers.

Also found in other woods, *Russula ochroleuca* is so-called after the colour of its sunken cap, which ranges in colour from straw-yellow or lemon-yellow to ochre. It has wide, delicate gills, which are white initially and then become straw-coloured. The stalk is solid at first, becoming spongy, slightly swollen towards the base, and, in fully grown specimens, reticulate and striate on a greyish-white background. The flesh is white or slightly yellowish beneath the cuticle. It is not very scented, but bitter and this species should not be eaten.

Russula vesca, on the other hand, is edible. It is not bitter or acrid, but is nevertheless not greatly prized. This fungus can be identified by the cap, which eventually becomes sunken, is a fairly deep flesh colour, and has a striate margin. The gills are white and ooze a milky liquid which, when exposed to the air, turns slightly rust-coloured. The stalk is solid with shading of the same colour as the cap. The flesh is white and does not smell. It is commonly found in summer and autumn in larch and beech woods.

Russula caerulea has a cap 5–10 centimetres in diameter, which is initially convex with a central umbo. As the fungus matures, the cap becomes depressed but humped in the centre, slightly viscous, and fairly deep

Above: Gomphidius rutilus usually grows alone
Above centre: Hygrophorus eburneus has decurrent gills and an umbo
Above left: Tricholoma flavovirens is an edible species with a mealy smell

bluish-violet in colour. The stalk is quite slender and is white. The flesh is also white and when raw has a sweetish taste, which turns acrid on cooking. Although not poisonous, it should not be eaten.

Russula queletii somewhat resembles the closely related *Russula sardonia*. It has a violet, convex and then depressed cap, with initially white and then straw-coloured gills. The stalk is tapered and whitish with shades of the same colour as the cap. It is acrid, however, and not worth eating. *Russula sardonia* is found in pine woods and is distinguished from *Russula queletii* largely on the basis of chemical tests.

Russula xerampelina is another reddish species which varies considerably in its cap colour and is found in woods generally. Its flesh is not peppery. In conifer woods one often comes across *Russula erythropoda*, which is sometimes considered only to be a variety of the *xerampelina* species. It is edible and may be identified by the slightly depressed cap which is crimson-red and slightly darker at the centre, and by the gills which are a pretty straw-yellow colour and develop brown patches in very mature specimens. The stalk is cylindrical, regular, pinkish-red (somewhat lighter at the base) and sometimes faded on one of the surfaces. The whitish flesh has a particular smell of cooked prawns, especially in not so young specimens.

Russula turci, also an edible species, is found in a wide range of conifer woodlands. The cap is convex, then flat and finally depressed. With a diameter of 3–8 centimetres, it is slimy when the climate is damp and purplish-violet, often darker at the centre and sometimes with yellowish markings. The gills are set quite widely apart, cream-coloured, becoming ochre-coloured latterly. The usually short stalk is delicate and white, and the flesh is white and sweetish, with a smell of iodine at the base of the stalk.

Russula nauseosa is a small species quite frequently found in damp conifer woods. The cap is a mixture of brown and purple in colour, while the gills are deep yellow. The stalk is white and slender. Another *Russula* species of wet conifer woods is *Russula paludosa.* It is not very common and occurs mainly with *Sphagnum,* the peat-moss. It is a striking species, with a shiny, brick red cap,

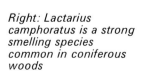
Above: This natural spruce wood is rather more open and rich in its fungi than closely-packed forestry plantations

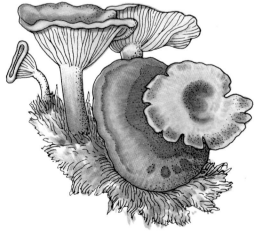

Right: Lactarius camphoratus is a strong smelling species common in coniferous woods

creamy gills and a stout, rust-tinged stalk. *Russula puellaris* has a purple-pink cap, pale yellow gills and a yellowish stalk. It is a small species, no more than five centimetres in diameter.

The Milk Caps
Some species of Milk Cap are particularly common in conifer woods, in particular *Lactarius deliciosus, Lactarius sanguifluus, Lactarius rufus, Lactarius mitissimus, Lactarius camphoratus, Lactarius helvus* and *Lactarius scrobiculatus,* the last of which has been described earlier.

The Saffron Milk Cap (*Lactarius deliciosus*) is without any doubt one of the most typical fungi of coniferous woodland and also one of the best. It is very easily identifiable, being of average size with a slightly irregular cap which quickly becomes sunken. It is light brick-coloured with darker concentric zones, tending to reddish or pale red. The gills and stalk are the same colour as the cap and all the various parts of the fungus develop rather unattractive bluish-green patches if touched. The principal feature of this fungus is that its flesh, which is whitish in the inner part, oozes a bright orange-coloured 'milk' which turns greenish when exposed to the air. The aptly named *Lactarius sanguifluus,* a rare species, is very closely related to the above species, differing only in having darker red shading and a deep blood-red milk.

Lactarius rufus, however, is quite different. It is a more slender shape, with a cap of a uniform red-brown colour. This is umbonate initially, and then funnel-shaped, with conspicuous rounding at the bottom. The gills range from straw-yellow to ochre-coloured, and the stalk is paler than the cap. The reddish-white flesh oozes a white milk which is at first mild but later very acrid. It is commonly found during the autumn in various types of conifer wood, and considered suspect and even poisonous.

Lactarius mitissimus is smaller, and found generally in conifer woods. It is edible but very poor tasting. Its cap passes from being brick-coloured to orange, and it has cream-coloured gills. The stalk is the same colour as the cap or slightly lighter. The flesh is yellowish, with a pleasant smell and has a taste which is sweet at first and then very peppery. It oozes a slightly bitter white milk.

Lactarius camphoratus – the camphor-scented Milk Cap – is so-called after the smell of sweet clover and fenugreek which is emitted by its reddish, sweetish flesh. Of average size, its cap is initially convex, then flat and finally slightly concave. It remains round-topped at all stages and is reddish-brown in colour with a striate-fluted margin. The gills are brownish-red and decurrent. The stalk is fairly slender, rugose, that is, wrinkled and rough, and the same colour as the cap, or darker. It is edible but again has a very poor taste.

A fungus of wet places under conifers is *Lactarius helvus.* Gills and stalk are the same colour as the cap, which is coffee or cinnamon. The cap is covered with small scales and expanded. It is a tasteless species with a watery milk.

The Tricholoma fungi
The following species of the genus *Tricholoma* occur in conifer woods: *Tricholoma rutilans, Tricholoma colossus, Tricholoma flavovirens, Tricholoma orirubens, Tricholoma albobrunnea, Tricholoma saponaceum, Tricholoma pessundatum, Tricholoma aurantium, Tricholoma terreum, Tricholoma virgatum, Tricholoma psammopus, Tricholoma imbricatum* and *Tricholoma portentosum.* The first species, better known as *Tricholomopsis rutilans,* has a very distinctive cap which has purple-brown patches or dots on a yellow background; the gills are also yellow, as is the stalk, which has reddish shading. The flesh is yellowish. It grows on wood, and is common in all types of coniferous woodlands. It is edible but poor tasting and some consider it suspect or even poisonous.

Tricholoma colossus is larger and squat; it is an edible species and is conserved in oil in some countries. The cap is initially hemispherical, and eventually becomes slightly convex, with margins that are markedly curled towards the gills which are red-brown in colour. The gills are very close together, white, and patched with areas of a light reddish colour in adult specimens. The stalk is squat, white in the upper part and the same colour as the cap lower down. The very firm flesh is white and becomes flesh-coloured when exposed to the air.

Tricholoma flavovirens is of average size, less squat than the *colossus* species, and

Above: The Chantarelle
is one of the most
highly-prized edible
fungi
Right: Rozites caperata
is a rare species

Below Cortinarius
purpurascens
Below right: Tricholoma
aurantium is often
found in groups or fairy
rings

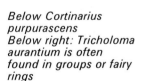

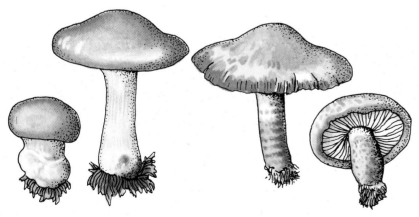

coloured all over a light sulphur-yellow. Against the background colour the cap has a reddish area at the centre and small reddish scales. The flesh is white, straw-coloured beneath the cuticle, and is faintly scented with a sweet taste. This is a good quality edible species, but can be confused with *Tricholoma sulphureum,* which has been mentioned earlier. The latter species, however, is restricted to broadleaf woods, especially oak, while the former is found in sandy pine woods.

In many respects *Tricholoma pessundatum,* another species already described, is very akin to *Tricholoma albobrunneum,* differing principally in size. *Tricholoma pessundatum* is the larger fungus and has a sturdier shape with a stalk which does not differ much in colour in the lower and upper parts. The *pessundatum* species is not poisonous but its flesh has a bitter taste. It is, of course, found not only in pine woods but also in broadleaf woods and even in poplar woods.

Tricholoma orirubens calls to mind *Tricholoma terreum,* with its grey cap and small darker scales. It differs from the *terreum* species in that its flesh turns red when exposed to the air. Its stalk also tends to be bluish at the base where one can see small tufts of yellow, felt-like mycelium. *Tricholoma terreum* itself is a predominantly coniferous species.

A rare species, *Tricholoma aurantium* (= *Armillaria aurantia*) is a handsome fungus with a cap that is orange tending to reddish-brown. Its stalk has scales which rise from the base and form a sort of incomplete ring. In terms of edibility, it is only mediocre because its flesh emits an unpleasant smell.

Two other Tricholomas with dark caps are *Tricholoma portentosum* and *Tricholoma virgatum.* The former has a greyish-brown colour to the cap, yellowish gills and a stout stalk covered with fibrous strands. This is found in sandy pine woods. The second species is darker in colour, with a somewhat conical cap and a tall, white stalk. It is found generally in conifer woods, unlike *Tricholoma imbricatum,* which is confined to pine trees. This species is similarly conical, but reddish-brown in colour. Slightly smaller in size and lighter in colour is *Tricholoma psammopus,* which is confined to larch woods.

Other conifer fungi

Apart from the genera such as those above, which are well represented in coniferous woodland, there are many which only have one or two species present. A viscous species of *Cortinarius* is *Cortinarius mucosus*, which has a light red-brown cap, tending to orange at the margin. The cap is very slimy, as is the lower part of the stalk, where it is light brown and scaly. The top of the stalk, on the other hand, is white and has a ring formed by the remnants of the veil which previously protected the gills. The flesh is whitish, sweet at first, and in mature specimens slightly peppery. It is not poisonous, but only of mediocre quality.

Conifer woods also harbour *Cortinarius purpurascens*, which is found in other woods. Rather squat and of average size, this species has a cap 8–14 centimetres in diameter, and is fleshy, convex and then almost flat. Its cap is slightly viscous and reddish-brown in colour tending to violet, often with markings. The gills are bluish and develop purplish wine-coloured patches if touched. The stalk is swollen at the base and bulbous, and also bluish-violet. The flesh of this edible species is compact, violet, whitish in adult specimens, with a slight but pleasant smell and a particularly distinctive taste.

Cortinarius collinitus, another edible species, is similar to *Cortinarius mucosus* and, like the *mucosus* species, has a viscous stalk. Its cap, which is slimy, differs in being lighter at the margin. The gills are close together, whitish at first and streaked with violet, and then ochreous rust-coloured. The stalk is like that of *Cortinarius mucosus* with a similar white veil at the top in young specimens. It has wart-like scales below, left over from the veil and showing brown-ochre shades.

Gomphidius rutilus is another slimy fungus common in pine woods. This highly distinctive species is slender, with a conically bell-shaped cap initially, which later becomes convex and umbonate. This cap is red-brown in colour and usually streaked with violet wine-coloured shades. The gills are slightly lighter in colour than the cap, while the stalk is solid, tapered towards the base, and the same colour as the cap. The flesh is flesh-coloured, yellowish in the stalk, does not smell greatly, and has a pleasant

taste. It is an edible summer and autumn fungus.

Paxillus atrotomentosus, which sometimes grows to a considerable size, is found on conifer stumps. The cap (8–30 centimetres in diameter) is fleshy, convex and then irregularly flattened, and chamois-ochre in colour. The gills are decurrent, anastomosed (fused) at the base and ochre-coloured. The stalk is squat, often eccentric and even lateral, as in species of *Pleurotus*. It is blackish and velvety in appearance. The flesh of this species, which is not edible, is very firm, whitish and bitter.

The Chantarelle

An edible and very well-known fungus which is locally common in both conifer and broad-leaf woods is the Chantarelle (*Cantharellus cibarius*). It is small or of average size with a cap which eventually turns slightly concave and is irregularly lobed at the margin. The cap is bright yellow above and lighter coloured below, where one can observe pleats or folds which look like gills. These are, however, thicker than gills, ramified or anastomosed and decurrent to the stalk. The stalk itself is slightly tapered towards the base and the same colour as the lower surface of the cap. The flesh is firm and yellowish. It is used at the table as a condi-

Above: A larch wood species, Boletus elegans is edible and has a pronounced ring on its stalk

Above: The larch is one of the few deciduous conifers. It is widely planted in Britain for its timber

Below: Hygrophorus lucorum is a small autumnal fungus found in larch woods

ment for flavouring and needs to be well cooked.

The rare *Rozites caperata* is found in a wide range of woods, especially if they are not too damp, and have a sandy soil. The cap, which is 6–10 centimetres in diameter, is rounded to egg-shaped at first, then convex, and fairly deep ochre-yellow in colour. It is grooved and striate at the margin, showing the remains of the overall silvery-white veil in young specimens. The gills are straw-coloured, then ochreous, and finally denticulate (with little teeth). The stalk is cylindrical, striate and tomentose, or downy, at the top and has a membranous, striate ring. The overall colour is straw-like or whitish. The flesh of this species is edible.

Among the smallest and most interesting of conifer wood fungi, *Panellus* (= *Pleurotus*) *mitis*, is only one or two centimetres across, with a minute, flattened stalk. Both cap and lateral stalk are pale flesh-coloured when mature, but completely white when young. This species is particularly found on spruce trees.

Among the *Hygrophorus* group is *Hygrophorus eburneus*, an ivory-white species, so called because of its colour. Its cap is 3–6 centimetres in diameter, and also very slimy. The gills are white and set far apart. The white, slimy stalk is slightly granulose at the top and the flesh is not scented and has no taste. *Hygrophorus cossus*, a variety

similar to the edible *eburneus* species, is also common. Although they are alike in shape and colour, the *cossus* species is identifiable by its unpleasant smell. This scent resembles that of the large larvae of an insect, *Cossus cossus*, which is harmful to the trunks of numerous species of trees.

A fungus typical of larch wood is *Hygrophorus lucorum*, a small edible species found in autumn. The cap is convex-umbonate at first, then flat and slightly depressed, and a fine yellow in colour. The gills are distant, slightly decurrent, ranging from white to yellowish in colour. The stalk is slender, cylindrical and hollow. It is white in colour, streaked with yellow, as is the flesh, which has no specific taste or smell.

On some soils, broadleaf species grow close to conifers, forming mixed woodland, and causing great confusion in the mushroom hunter's mind. Symbiotic fungi often grow some distance from their tree partners, and so a 'conifer' fungus species may spring up under an oak tree 100 metres away from the nearest conifer.

Conifers are also susceptible to fire, which has a dramatic effect on the fungus flora. Species such as the Charcoal Toadstool (*Pholiota carbonaria*) are associated with burnt conifer stumps. This burnt ground becomes in effect, temporary heathland, allowing many 'alien' fungi of open ground to invade the preserve of woodland fungi.

Fungi of Heath and Moorland

Although they have distinct names, and are often thought of in rather different terms, heaths and moors are effectively one and the same thing. Both are dominated by heathers of one sort or another and are apparently barren, windswept places. In spite of this, there is often a wide variety of plant life, including fungi. There are many factors which contribute to the formation and maintenance of heaths, including high winds, fires, grazing and tree felling. Otherwise, heaths and moors would eventually progress to woodland.

The Puffballs

The absence of any significant tree cover means that fungi of heaths and moors are mainly non-symbiotic and exist on humus, dead branches, leaves and manure. The fungi found in this habitat are for the most part small in size, with some exceptions. One such exception, and a truly remarkable one, is the Giant Puffball (*Lycoperdon = Calvatia giganteum*), a member of the Gasteromycetes, which also grows in other grassy places. The fruit-bearing bodies of this species are, when fully grown, extremely large. They may easily reach the size of a human head and much larger specimens have been found. They are spherical, slightly irregular, and greyish-white in colour. Inside, the flesh is white at first, gradually becoming pithy and passing to olive-yellow and eventually to greenish-brown. The flesh degenerates eventually into a dark powdery mass, consisting of thousands of millions of spores. Young specimens of this Puffball are edible, when the flesh is still white and firm.

The other species of Puffball are much smaller. Most are meadowland or woodland species, but *Lycoperdon ericetorum* is another heathland type. It is only 1–3 centimetres across and has no well-defined stalk, unlike most Puffballs. It is greyish-white or yellowish-brown in colour.

The Agarics

Laccaria laccata is a small Agaric common in woods and on heaths. It is 2–6 centimetres high, with a cap that is at first convex, then more or less flat. It remains umbilicate, that is, depressed locally, at the centre and striate at the margin. The colour varies from reddish-pink to brick- or cinnamon-coloured.

Above: Fungi are to be found even in hilly and mountainous districts
Below: Lycoperdon perlatum has pointed warts interspersed with granules (shown under magnification)

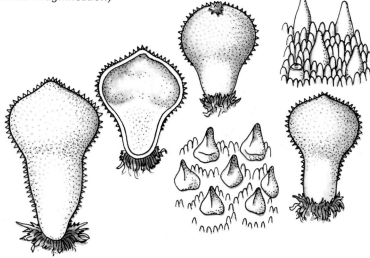

Above: In poor or exposed places, fungi can be found growing on or near animal manure
Above left: Laccaria laccata is commonly found on heaths, but also in woods
Left: A group of Lycoperdon perlatum, which is a species common in woods generally

The gills, which are set well apart and irregular, are slightly decurrent, ochre-pink or pale flesh-coloured, and eventually white because of the spores. The stalk is very slender, cylindrical, and the same colour as the cap. It is edible, but it is advisable to discard the stalks, which are fibrous. The *laccata* species has a relation, *Laccaria amethystina,* which is a woodland fungus.

Other small Agarics include several *Mycena* species, notably *Mycena leucogala.* This is a slender, shiny species with a parabolic cap which is dark brown or blackish. There are also several *Inocybe* species found on heaths. *Inocybe lacera* has a brown or olive-tinged cap 2–4 centimetres in diameter, which is slightly umbonate, and a short stalk which tapers. This is a poisonous species, in common with many other Inocybes. The gills are distant and brownish when mature. *Inocybe casimiri* has a longer stalk which is covered in small scales. It is generally darker in colour than *Inocybe lacera.*

Among the slightly larger Agarics are *Hygrophorus conicus* and two *Clitocybe* species. *Hygrophorus conicus* has a cap which is cone-shaped, irregular and lobate. It is often larger on one side than the other, sometimes grooved, glabrous (free of hair) and slightly damp and viscous. Its colour varies from lemon-yellow to orange and may even be blackish in more mature specimens. The gills are white with a yellow margin and pass to greenish and eventually blackish. The stalk is cylindrical, slender, delicate and the same colour as the cap. The white flesh, which is yellow beneath the skin, has little taste. Most mycologists treat this as an edible fungus, but there are those who regard it as suspect and even poisonous.

Clitocybe infundibuliformis, as its specific name suggests, is funnel-shaped, 4–8 centimetres in diameter, and flesh or leather-coloured. The gills are white and decurrent, while the stalk is lighter than the cap and swollen at the base. The smaller *Clitocybe langei* also has a depressed cap, but the decurrent gills are grey-brown and the stalk is more slender. This is a species of heaths and woods, associated with birch species and bracken.

In a similar habitat to the last species, one may also find, in groups, a small species,

Hebeloma mesophaeum. The cap of this fungus is not fleshy, and 2–4 centimetres in diameter. It is initially convex and rounded, but becomes flat, reddish-brown, and lighter at the margin, where one finds the remnants of the partial veil in the form of white, cotton-like fringes. The gills are close together, whitish in colour initially, passing to bistre. The stalk also bears the remains of the partial veil, being brownish and fibrillose, while the flesh is pale brown, with little smell and a slightly bitter taste. All Hebelomas are best regarded as suspect, as some are poisonous.

This applies, of course, to another Hebeloma found in this habitat. Fairy Cakes (*Hebeloma crustuliniforme*) is larger than the previous species and is a light whitish-brown in colour. Unlike the related *mesophaeum* species, it has no veil and has a much shorter, stouter stalk than other Hebelomas. The cap is slightly sticky and the flesh has a smell of radishes, which is a useful characteristic for identification. This fungus is found in late summer and autumn on heathland and sometimes in woods and gardens.

The Horsehair Fungus (*Marasmius androsaceus*) has a cap about a centimetre in diameter, growing on a prominent black mycelium and with a black stalk. The cap is wrinkled and the gills are distant.

The False Chantarelle

Heathland is one of the habitats of the False Chantarelle (*Hygrophoropsis = Cantharellus = Clitocybe aurantiaca*). This edible species may be confused with the true Chantarelle, but is generally a brighter colour, orange-yellow, and lacks the smell of apricots possessed by the Chantarelle.

A striking but small Polypore of burnt heathland is *Coltrichia perennis.* It is stalked, but cap and stalk merge in a funnel shape. Inside the funnel the cap is zoned and hairy, and the entire fungus is leathery and deep brown. Still more unusual, though common, is a species, *Thelephora terrestris,* which is related to the 'crust' fungi found on wood. This species grows up to eight centimetres in diameter and lacks the usual appearance of most fungi. The fruiting body is composed of fan-shaped and fringed, dark brown funnels which are extremely fibrillous. It occurs in clusters on heathy soils and among conifers.

Glossary

Acrid Describes the taste of the flesh or milk of fungi, usually belonging to the genera *Russula* and *Lactarius;* this taste is acid and burns, and may irritate the mucous membranes in the mouth and in the digestive system.

Agaric The generic term used to denote fungi which have gills beneath the cap.

Alveolate Describes the mitre-shaped cap of fungi, in particular the Morels (genus *Morchella*), and denotes their honeycomb-like structure.

Anastomosed Describes the gills or similar elements on the lower surface of the cap of many fungi (e.g. the Chantarelle, genus *Cantharellus*) when they are joined together to form a kind of network.

Angular Describes the pores under the cap of certain Boletes which, instead of being round, have a less regular, hence angular, outline.

Areolate A surface broken up into numerous small areas, separated by cracks etc.

Ascospore These are the spores, of sexual origin, produced inside the ascus.

Ascus A microscopic organ peculiar to the Ascomycetes (e.g. Morels, Truffles), spherical, club-shaped, oblong or cylindrical in shape, inside which are produced usually four, but sometimes more, spores.

Attenuated Describes a fruiting body or other organ which is round in cross-section, longitudinally elongate, not quite cylindrical but somewhat tapered, towards one end.

Autotrophe Any organism capable of synthesizing sugars from the carbon dioxide in the air and the water in the substratum, using, as energy, sunlight (photosynthesis); fungi are not autotrophic, whereas all green plants are.

Basidiospore These are the spores, of sexual origin, which form on the outside of the basidium and are carried by it.

Basidium This is a single-celled or, more rarely, a multiple-celled structure typical of the Basidiomycetes. Externally it bears one to four spores (basidiospores); it is usually club-shaped, occasionally spherical or elongated.

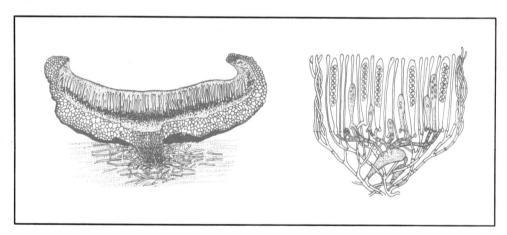

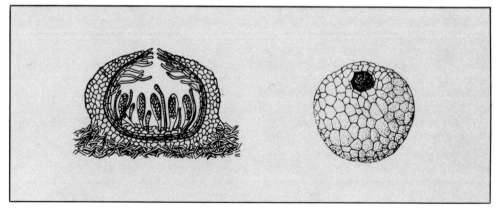

Above right: A fruiting body with (right) an enlarged detail
Right: This is the fruiting body, in section (left) and many times magnified, of a minute Ascomycete, commonly found in bark or in dung

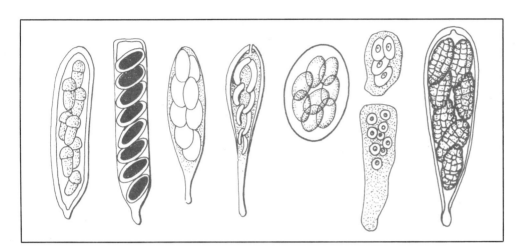

*Left: Various types of asci and their spores
Below left: A basidium with four basidio-spores at the tips of the horns (sterigmata)*

Bifurcate Forked—applied to gills which are divided (e.g. certain species of the genus *Russula*).

Boletes Fungi characterized by a stalk attached centrally to a cap which has tubules ending, on the lower surface, in pores.

Bulbous Describes the stalk of fungi when it is basally swollen like a bulb (e.g. the Death Cap and many species of the genus *Cortinarius*).

Bracket fungi Popular name denoting the corticolous fungi of the genus *Polyporus* and similar genera which grow in the shape of a bracket.

Campanulate Bell shape formed by the cap of many fungi at a certain stage in development (e.g. certain types of *Coprinus, Hygrophorus* etc.).

Cap or pileus The wide upper structure found in the majority of the higher fungi, beneath which there may be gills (as in Agarics), pores (Boletes and species of *Polyporus*) or spines (species of *Hydnum*).

Carpophore Fruiting body.

Caustic Describes the milk secreted by certain fungi in the genera *Lactarius* and *Russula* when the taste burns and irritates.

Citrine Lemon-yellow, or may sometimes indicate a colour somewhat paler than lemon (e.g. *Amanita citrina*).

Concolorous Having the same colour e.g. when the gills or stem are the same colour as the cap.

Conical Of the cap when the shape of the upper surface is convex: half way between spherical and flat.

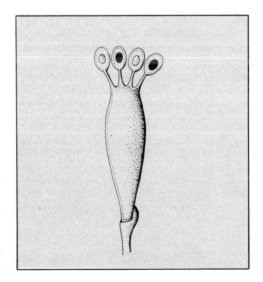

Coriaceous Of the flesh of fungi when the texture is leathery.

Corticolous Of fungi which grow on the bark of tree-trunks, sometimes in the shape of a bracket (or shelf), sometimes in the shape of a hoof, and sometimes like conventional mushrooms.

Cortina The veil which, in many young fungi, stretches from the margin of the cap to the upper or central part of the stalk. It is thread-like and silky or cobwebby, and is well-developed in species belonging to the genus *Cortinarius*.

Costate Having ribs. May apply to the cap or the stalk.

Crowded Of the gills when they are close together.

Cuticle Also termed epidermis or pellicle— the thin skin which covers the cap of fungi.

Right: Cap shapes in fungi—1 flat, 2 concave, 3 infundibuliform, 4 convex, 5 hemispherical, 6 conical, 7 ovoid, 8 truncated, 9 umbonate, 10 involute, 11 revolute
Below right: The gleba of a Gasteromycete

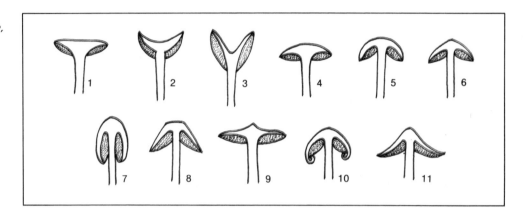

Decurrent Of the gills when they extend from the cap of a fungus to the stalk. Also applies to the tubules of certain Boletes and species of *Polyporus*.

Depressed Describes the cap of a fungus when the upper surface is more or less concave.

Discomycete Cup Fungus (e.g. *Peziza* species), where the fruiting body is cup-shaped, with the hymenium on the upper surface.

Distant A term applied to gills when they are well spaced (opposite of 'crowded').

Eccentric Describes the stalk of a fungus when it is attached slightly off-centre to the cap.

Elastic Of the flesh of a fungus when its texture is elastic, or pliable.

Epidermis See Cuticle.

Fairy rings Colonies of fungi sometimes grow in circles especially in grassy places because of the way the mycelium grows and occurs, especially in certain species of the genus *Tricholoma*.

Fibrils These are the very fine filaments which may be seen running lengthwise down the stalk of certain fungi, or, more often, radiating across the cap.

Fibrous refers to the stalk of a fungus which, when broken, shows a longitudinal, fibrillar structure (e.g. the Honey Fungus).

Fimicolous Of fungi growing on dung or manure.

Floccose Of structures like small scales or warts which are soft and downy and may appear on the ring, stalk or cap.

Fluted or grooved Describes the cap of a fungus when it has grooves at the margin.

Fovea Small shallow broad pit, usually irregular, on the stalk of certain fungi.

Free Of gills which are not joined to the stalk.

Fusiform Spindle-shaped, applied to the stalk of fungi when it is tapered. Also describes spores which have this shape as seen under the microscope.

Gibbous Humped—of the cap of a fungus when it has swellings or lumps.

Gills The blade-like strips of tissue arranged radially around the stalk beneath the cap.

Gleba The fertile or spore-containing part of fungi with spherical bodies, applied to the Gasteromycetes (e.g. Puffballs).

Granulose Covered with small granules, as in the upper part of the stalk of *Boletus granulatus*.

Grooved Of the stalk or cap of a fungus when it has fairly regular and numerous grooves.

Heterotrophe Any organism obliged to feed on already processed substances, or

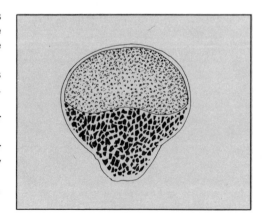

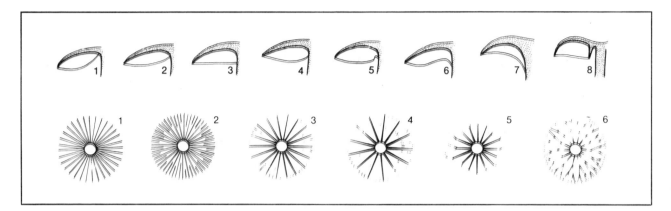

substances already synthesised by other organisms. It applies to all higher fungi.

Hymenium The fertile layer which contains or carries the spores. In addition to the asci or basidia contained, there are also various sterile cells known as paraphyses and cystidia.

Hypha Individual filament of the mycelium and fruiting body, composed of cells laid end to end.

Inedible Of a fungus which is not good to eat, although it may often be non-poisonous.
Infundibuliform Funnel-shaped.
Intermediate Of gills which do not extend completely from the cap edge to the stalk. Particularly common in species of *Mycena* and *Lactarius*.
Involute Describes the margin of the cap of fungi when it is clearly curled inwards.

Lacunose Describes the stalk when it has internal cavities which are usually unequal and random.
Lateral Refers to a stalk attached to one side of the cap.
Latex or milk. The fairly thick, sticky liquid secreted by the flesh of Milk Caps.
Lobate Describes the cap of a fungus when the outline is uneven and has lobes.

Macromycetes The larger fungi, whose structure is visible to the naked eye.
Mealy Describes a surface covered by a very fine layer of powdery matter, like flour.
Medullary Pithy, refers to the consistency of the flesh inside the stalk.
Micromycetes Microscopic fungi, usually parasitic or saprophytic on vegetable or animal organs.

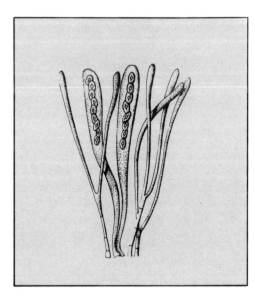

Milk See Latex.
Mitre Specific name given to the cap of numerous Ascomycetes (genera *Morchella*, *Gyromitra*), which resembles a papal mitre in shape.
Mobile Of the ring which, when fully developed, and still entire, may move along the stalk (e.g. Parasol Mushroom).
Mycelium This is the complex of microscopic filaments (hyphae) which form the first stage of development of a fungus; it may be cobwebby, or felt-like in appearance, or strap- or string-shaped. In particular conditions the mycelium produces fruit-bearing bodies.
Mycorrhiza A fungal tissue composed of hyphae enveloping young tree roots either on their surface (ectotrophic mycorrhiza) or by penetrating them (endotrophic mycorrhiza).

Above: Types of gill attachment (top)— 1 free, 2 adnexed, 3 adnate, 4 sinuate, 5 emarginate, 6 uncinate, 7 decurrent, 8 inserted on a collar; and patterns of gill arrangement (bottom)— 1 equal, 2–4 unequal, 5 furcate, 6 branched Left: Paraphyses are sterile hyphae within the hymenium

Right: Two mushrooms with pores on the underside of the cap. The inset shows the shape of the pores
Below right: The sclerotium of Claviceps purpurea, showing numerous fruiting bodies

Obtuse Of the apex of a cap when it is fairly rounded or truncate.
Ovoid Egg-shaped.

Partial veil The delicate membrane which, in many young fungi, stretches from the margin of the cap to the stalk and protects the gills. As the fungus grows, the partial veil tears to form the ring, sometimes leaving traces on the margin of the cap.
Plicate A pleated margin.
Polypore A fungus with pores beneath the cap, usually sessile or with a short, lateral stalk. Distinguished from Boletes by the pores being strongly attached to the flesh.
Pores The orifices of the tubules in the Polypores and Boletes.
Pruinose A slight waxy or powdery appearance.

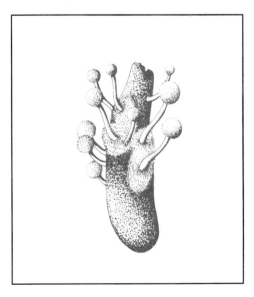

Ramified Of the gills and similar parts beneath the cap of many fungi which rather than being decurrent are branched or ramified (e.g. the Chantarelle).
Reticulate A specific mesh pattern of varying colours which decorates the top of the stalk of numerous Boletes.
Rhizomorph A root-like form of mycelium found in fungi such as the Honey Fungus.
Rib An elongate, ridge-like protuberance. The caps or stalks of certain ribbed fungi are termed costate.
Ring This is the soft or membranous remnant of the partial veil which encircles the upper part of the stalk.

Saprophyte Any organism which feeds off dead or decaying animal or plant material.
Scabrous Of the stalk when it has fairly pronounced rough areas, sometimes in the form of irregular granulations, sometimes as scales.
Scale A particle found on the cap of Agarics, being the remains of the universal veil. As in many Amanitas. The stalk of some species can also be scaly.
Sclerotium A resting body for tiding a fungus over unfavourable conditions, found in a wide variety of fungi, particularly the Rusts and Smuts.
Scrobiculate Of stalks which have shallow, broad, pits.
Separate Of gills which may be simply separate, or set well apart. Also describes the gills when free from the stalk.
Septum A partition, found in hyphae, dividing them into interconnected compartments.
Sessile Having no stalk.

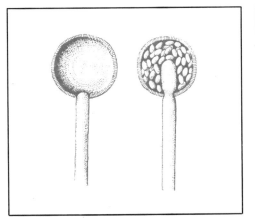

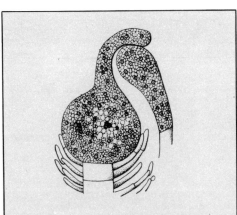

Far left: A sporangium and a sectional view (right) showing the asexual spores
Left: These are specialized sexual hyphae, greatly magnified, which will fuse, eventually producing sexual spores
Below left: A selection of fungal spores

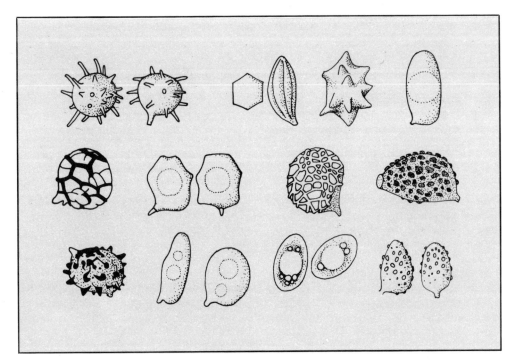

Spines The delicate, sharp-pointed appendages which cover the lower surface of the cap of fungi belonging to the family *Hydnaceae*.

Spore A cell of sexual or asexual origin capable of germinating and producing an organism similar to the one which produced it.

Squamous Of the cap or stalk of a fungus when it is covered with scales.

Sterigma Pointed tips of the fertile cells (basidia) of the Basidiomycetes. Each sterigma bears a basidiospore. There are between one and four to each basidium.

Stipe Stalk.

Striae Very fine lines, silky in appearance, arranged radially and close together on the cap of many fungi, especially species of the genera *Russula, Tricholoma* and *Cortinarius*.

Stroma Fungal tissue which is not itself reproductive, but may bear reproductive structures such as conidia and perithecia.

Suberose Of the flesh of fungi when it has a cork-like texture.

Substratum Anything (e.g. earth, bark, wood) on which fungi and other organisms grow.

Symbiont A fungus or any other vegetable or animal organism which grows in symbiosis.

Right: A conidiophore of one of the Fungi Imperfecti, showing the chains of conidia
Below right: A typical Agaric in various stages, showing the universal and partial veils. The raised warts are the remnants of the universal veil
Bottom right: The volva in many Amanitas is pronounced. It ruptures to leave a jagged 'sac' at the base

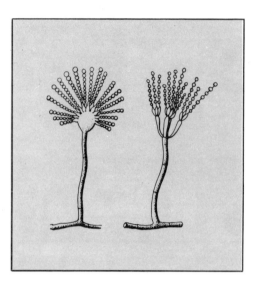

Ventricose Of the stalk of a fungus when it bulges in the middle.
Verrucose Of the cap of a fungus when the surface has warts.
Viscid Of the cap or stalk of a fungus when it is moist and slimy, but not sticky.
Viscous Of the cap or stalk of a fungus when it is moist and sticky to the touch.
Volva A membranous basal structure containing the base of the stalk of certain fungi.

Warts Fragments on the cap of many fungi, as remnants of the universal veil.

Zonate Describes the caps of many fungi, especially of the genus *Lactarius,* when they have a sequence of alternate concentric zones of varying colours.

Symbiosis An association between two organisms belonging to different species, in which a very close relationship is formed.

Teleutospore A resting spore of the Rusts and Smuts.
Thermolabile Of fungal poisons which, when heated to at least 60°C, lose most or all of their toxicity.
Tomentose Of the surface of the cap or stipe of fungi when they are hairy or downy.
Tomentum A covering formed by short hairs.
Trama Inner tissue of the gill in Agarics.
Trilobate Of the caps of certain Helvellas, which, when seen from above, have three fairly symmetrical lobes.
Tuberculate Of the margin of the caps in certain fungi (e.g. *Russula foetens*), which have a series of small protuberances or tubercles.
Tubule Minute tubular structures peculiar to pore fungi (Boletes and *Polyporus* species). The tubules are gathered together in a mass, parallel and vertical, and form the lower part of the cap of the above-mentioned fungi.

Umbo A pronounced swelling at the centre of the cap of numerous fungi which are therefore called umbonate.
Universal veil The membrane which, in many fungi, covers the whole body of the young fungus. As the fungus develops, it tears to form the volva (e.g. in the Death Cap).

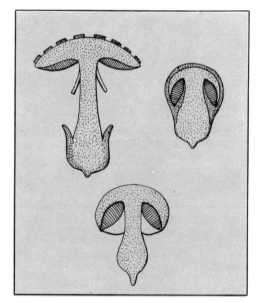

An Ecological Guide to Fungi

This index is designed to summarize and extend the species covered in the main part of the book. It shows at a glance the different species that occur together, as well as the wide range of some fungi. Although many fungi species are particularly associated with one tree species, there are many borderline cases which are matters of dispute. So the table acts not as an infallible record, so much as a reflection of the consensus. Furthermore, some species are mentioned more than once because they are found in more than one habitat or with more than one tree species.

For some reason, the fungi have attracted a great variety of common names, many of which are used only in certain regions. Common names are therefore given in preceding chapters, but are omitted in the tabular matter to ensure clarity.

FUNGI OF CULTIVATED AND HABITED PLACES

Armillaria mellea
Boletus leucophaeus (scaber)
Coprinus atramentarius
Coprinus comatus
Coprinus micaceus
Hypholoma fasciculare
Hypholoma sublateritium
Lyophyllum decastes
Marasmius oreades
Peziza spp
Phallus impudicus
Rhodophyllus sinuatus
Stropharia aeruginosa
Tricholoma nudum

FUNGI OF FIELDS AND MEADOWS

Agaricus arvensis
Agaricus bisporus
Agaricus campestris
Agaricus silvicola
Agaricus xanthoderma
Boletus impolitus
Boletus luridus
Clitocybe dealbata
Clitocybe rivulosa
Coprinus atramentarius
Coprinus comatus
Gyromitra esculenta
Gyromitra gigas
Helvella crispa
Helvella elastica
Helvella infula
Helvella lacunosa

Helvella monachella
Hygrophorus niveus
Hygrophorus puniceus
Lepiota badhami
Lepiota excoriata
Lepiota friesii
Lepiota gracilenta
Lepiota helveola
Lepiota leucothites
Lepiota procera
Lepiota rhacodes
Lycoperdon giganteum
Marasmius oreades
Morchella elata
Morchella esculenta
Morchella semi-libera
Morchella vulgaris
Pholiota mutabilis
Rhodophyllus dichrous
Rhodophyllus staurosporus
Verpa conica
Verpa digitaliformis

FUNGI OF BROADLEAF WOODS

General species. Species of more than one type of woodland.
Amanita rubescens
Amanita vaginata
Amanita virosa
Armillaria mellea
Armillaria tabescens
Boletus aurantiacus

Boletus calopus
Boletus chrysenteron
Boletus edulis
Boletus erythropus
Boletus impolitus
Boletus luridus
Boletus subtomentosus
Cantharellus cibarius
Clitocybe nebularis
Collybia fusipes
Collybia velutipes
Daedalea quercina
Hydnum repandum
Hydnum rufescens
Laccaria amethystina
Lactarius piperatus
Lactarius torminosus
Lactarius vellereus
Paxillus involutus
Pholiota praecox
Pholiota squarrosa
Pleurotus ostreatus
Polyporus squamosus
Rhodophyllus dichrous
Rhodophyllus nidorosus
Rhodophyllus sinuatus
Rhodophyllus staurosporus
Russula atropurpurea
Russula ochroleuca
Russula violacea
Tricholoma nudum
Tricholoma saponaceum
Tuber species
Volvariella bombycina

Birch

Amanita fulva
Amanita muscaria
Boletus leucophaeus (scaber)
Boletus parasiticus
Boletus testaceoscaber
Cortinarius armillatus
Cortinarius delibutus
Cortinarius flexipes
Cortinarius pholideus
Cortinarius semisanguineus
Lactarius scrobiculatus
Lactarius uvidus
Pholiota apicrea
Piptoporus betulinus
Russula claroflava
Russula nitida
Trametes betulina
Trametes cinnabarina
Tricholoma fulvum

Beech

Amanita citrina
Amanita excelsa
Amanita junquillea
Amanita pantherina
Amanita phalloides
Amanita vaginata
Boletus aereus
Boletus appendiculatus
Boletus aurata
Boletus chrysenteron
Boletus edulis
Boletus impolitus
Boletus olivacea
Boletus radicans
Boletus regius
Boletus satanas
Boletus subtomentosus
Collybia confluens
Collybia fusipes
Cortinarius albo-violaceus
Cortinarius calochrous
Cortinarius elatior
Cortinarius melleolens
Craterellus cornucopioides
Ganoderma applanatum
Inocybe fastigiata
Inocybe maculata
Inocybe patouillardii
Lactarius blennius
Lactarius fulvissimus
Lactarius pallidus
Lactarius subdulcis
Mycena–various species
Oudemansiella mucida
Oudemansiella radicata
Russula aurata
Russula cyanoxantha
Russula fellea
Russula lepida
Russula mairei
Russula olivacea
Russula rosea
Russula solaris
Russula virescens
Tricholoma argyraceum

Oak

Amanita citrina
Amanita phalloides
Collybia fusipes
Cortinarius albo-violaceus
Fistulina hepatica
Grifola frondosa
Lactarius quietus
Polyporus sulphureus

Russula vesca
Sclerotinia tuberosa

Elms   Pleurotus ulmarius
                    Polyporus squamosus

Elder   Auricularia auricula

Poplar   Boletus duriusculus
                    Pholiota destruens

Alder   Boletus lividus

FUNGI OF CONIFEROUS WOODS

General species. Species of
more than one type of conifer.
Many fungi are found in both
broadleaf and conifer woods.
Amanita citrina
Amanita excelsa
Amanita muscaria
Amanita porphyria
Amanita rubescens
Armillaria mellea
Armillaria tabescens
Boletus badius
Boletus calopus
Boletus erythropus
Boletus felleus
Boletus granulatus
Boletus luteus
Boletus piperatus
Boletus testaceoscaber
Boletus variegatus
Cantharellus cibarius
Clitocybe nebularis
Cortinarius collinitis
Hydnum rufescens
Hygrophoropsis aurantiaca
Lactarius camphoratus
Lactarius deliciosus
Lactarius mitissimus
Lactarius scrobiculatus
Paxillus atrotomentosus
Pholiota carbonaria
Russula emetica

Russula nauseosa
Russula ochroleuca
Russula paludosa
Russula puellaris
Russula queletii
Russula sanguinea
Russula xerampelina
Tricholoma albobrunnea
Tricholoma aurantium
Tricholoma rutilans
Tricholoma saponaceum
Tricholoma terreum
Tricholoma virgatum

Pines   Boletus bovinus
                    Boletus pinicola
                    Lactarius rufus
                    Russula sardonia
                    Tricholoma flavovirens
                    Tricholoma imbricatum
                    Tricholoma portentosum

Larch   Boletus elegans
                    Boletus tridentinus
                    Boletus viscidus

Spruce   Boletus cyanescens
                    Panellus mitis

FUNGI OF HEATHLAND AND MOORLAND

Amanita vaginata
Clavaria argillacea
Clitocybe infundibuliformis
Clitocybe langei
Coltrichia perennis
Hebeloma crustuliniforme
Hebeloma mesophaeum
Hygrophoropsis aurantiaca
Hygrophorus conicus
Inocybe casimiri
Inocybe lacera
Laccaria laccata
Lactarius torminosus
Lycoperdon ericetorum
Marasmius androsaceus
Mycera leucogala
Thelephora terrestris

Selected Bibliography

ALEXOPOULOS, C. J. *Introductory Mycology* (John Wiley, New York 1962; London 1965)

DENNIS, R. W. G. *British Cup Fungi and their Allies* Ray Society (British Museum, Natural History, London 1960)

DUDDINGTON, C. L. *Beginner's Guide to the Fungi* (Pelham Books, London 1972; Drake Publications, New York 1972)

FINDLAY, W. P. K. *Fungi, Wayside and Woodland Species* (F. Warne, London and New York 1967)

INGOLD, C. T. *Biology of Fungi* (Hutchinson Educational, London 1973)

KAVALER, L. *Mushrooms, Moulds and Miracles* (John Day, New York 1965; Harrap, London 1967)

LANGE, M. & HORA, F. B. *Guide to Mushrooms and Toadstools* (William Collins, Glasgow 1963; Dutton, New York 1976)

LARGE, E. C. *Advance of the Fungi* (Jonathan Cape, London 1940; Dover, New York 1940; Reprint—Peter Smith, Gloucester, Mass.)

PARKINSON, G. *Picture Information Book—Fungi* (A & C Black, London 1973)

RAMSBOTTOM, J. *Mushrooms and Toadstools* New Naturalist Series (William Collins, London and New York 1970)

SMITH, A. H. *The Mushroom Hunter's Field Guide* (University of Michigan Press, Ann Arbor 1971)

Acknowledgements

We are grateful to the following for permission to reproduce photographs on pages:

6 Flammulina velutipes (P. Pilloud/Jacana); 19 Ardea Photographics/D. W. Greenslade; 22 Bruce Coleman/S. C. Porter; 23 (top left) Archivio B, (top right) Jacana/A. Lanceau, (bottom) Bruce Coleman/S. C. Porter; 24 P2; 25 E.D.E.N.A.; 26 S. Viola (both); 28 E. Dulevant; 29 Titus; 30 Archivio B; 31 Bruce Coleman/ S. C. Porter; 33 (top) Bruce Coleman/S. C. Porter, (bottom) S. Viola; 34 S. Viola; 35 M. Pedone; 36 (top) S. Viola, (bottom) P2; 37 S. Viola; 38 S. Viola; 39 Marka; 40 S. Viola; 41 S. Viola; 42 F. Montacchini; 43 J. Six; 44 S. Viola (both); 45 (top) Jacana/H. Chaumeton; (bottom) Chiapponi; 46 Jacana/A. Adelbert; 47 (left) Jacana/H. Chaumeton, (right) P2; 48 A. Margiocco; 49 J. Six; 50 (top) C. Bevilacqua, (bottom) S. Viola; 51 P2; 52 Jacana/H. Chaumeton; 52–3 S. Viola; 53 J. Six; 55 E.D.E.N.A.; 56 Titus; 57 S. Viola (all); 58 J. Six; 63 J. Six; 65 (left) V. Pigazzini, (right top) S. Viola, (right bottom) P2; 67 P2; 69 Ardea Photographics; 70 (top) Jacana/H. Chaumeton, (centre and bottom) S. Viola; 71 Titus; 74–5 Archivio B; 76 Jacana/C. Carré; 77 Titus; 78 T. Schneiders; 79 G. Caproti; 80 (top left) F. Giovenzana, (top right) A. Mellano, (bottom) Jacana/H. Chaumeton.

Index